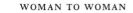

WOMAN TO WOMAN

Woman
to
Woman

by
Marguerite Duras
&
Xavière Gauthier

Les Parleuses   Translated and with an afterword

BY KATHARINE A. JENSEN

University of Nebraska Press: Lincoln & London

Originally published
as *Les Parleuses,*
© 1974 by Les Editions
de Minuit

The paper in this
book meets the minimum
requirements of
American National Stan-
dard for Information
Sciences – Permanence of
Paper for Printed
Library Materials,
ANSI Z39.48-1984

Library of Congress
Cataloging
in Publication Data

Duras, Marguerite.
Woman to woman.

(European women
writers series)

Translation of: Les
parleuses.

1. Duras, Marguerite–
Interviews. 2. Authors,
French–20th century–
Interviews.
I. Gauthier, Xavière.
II. Title. III. Series.
PQ2607.U8245Z46613 1987
843'.912   86-30796
ISBN 0-8032-1672-6
alkaline paper

Preface

We hesitated to publish these interviews in this way. We know we are taking a risk in leaving them *exactly as they were said*. They are teeming with repetitions and detours, with unfinished sentences left hanging or picked up again later in another mode or tone, with hiatus. The pace is slow, incredibly halting, then all at once extremely rapid. Our two discourses ride along side by side, trample on each other, interrupt, echo, harmonize, and disregard each other. Sometimes the words come out with difficulty and pain, and other times they rush out feverishly. It would have been easy—and it was tempting—to restructure the whole, to prune what seem like digressions from the dense brush of words, to force what is shooting off in all directions to go straight to the point, to straighten out this twisting, undulating crabwalk. To polish and police these interviews in order to regulate the grammar properly, to bend our thoughts to the rectitude of Cartesian logic. If we chose not to do this, it wasn't in the name of some Bergsonian principle of respect for real life, for the first rush of words, or for inspirational virginity. Rather, it's because this putting-in-order would have been an act of censorship and would have masked, as a result, what is undoubtedly the essential: that which is heard in the numerous silences, read in what was not said, in what was involuntarily screened and can be perceived in grammatical mistakes, in stylistic errors, and awkward expressions. The essential: what we didn't *want* to say but what was said without our knowing it, in the misfirings of clear, limpid, easy speech, in every slip of the tongue.

I believe that this refusal to organize and censor was especially important for these interviews for two reasons. First, because we are dealing with Marguerite Duras. And if there has ever been an oeuvre that allows so many rifts, gaps, and blanks to inscribe themselves unconsciously in the lives and acts of the "characters," it is certainly hers. The second reason is that both of us are women. If whole and well-established words have always been used, aligned, and stacked up by men, it is quite likely that the feminine might appear like the grass, which, at first a little wild and scraggly, manages to spring up between the chinks in old stones and ends up—why not?—breaking through the surface of cement slabs, no matter how heavy they may be, with the force of what has been long restrained. This may be one of the reasons these interviews risk appearing—to those who nostalgically long for words laid out neatly like cornfields (or battlefields)—like an inextricable jumble of creeper and ivy, an entanglement of climbing (or subterranean) plants.

And yet we have been obliged to lay out flat, on pages of writing, what should unfold like a fan—a constraint imposed by the fact that books are still read page by page. However, in listening to certain passages again, we sometimes felt like adding—since we didn't want to remove or cut out anything—something to or for or against or alongside what we'd said. We wanted, for example, to come back to one of the sentences of *L'Amour*[1]—"Isn't aware of being looked at"—which had attracted our attention at the beginning of the First Interview. Starting from there, we did the entire Fourth Interview, which should really be grafted onto the beginning of the book. We had to be satisfied with inscribing some reflections, spoken or written afterward, as if in the margins of the body of interviews [now in the Notes].

There were other times when, spellbound as I was by the discourse and person of Marguerite Duras, I didn't realize that the tape on the recorder had run out, and we had continued to speak without being recorded, sometimes for quite a while. The way we tried to retrieve what had been lost adds to the impression of a disjointedness, a hesitation, a spiraling line in the whole.

Finally, it might be useful to mention how these interviews originated. In May of 1973, I proposed to do a profile on writing by women for the paper *Le Monde*. The idea was accepted, and I interviewed women authors about their writing. Some refused to be interviewed; Julia Kristeva and Luce Irigaray agreed to write on the subject; Dominique Desanti and Marguerite Duras agreed to speak with me. When all the research and writing had been done and the spread was ready, *Le Monde* accepted it and scheduled publication for July of 1973. But then a major woman editor of the paper opposed the publication of the profile.

I had never met Marguerite Duras before. Her work had always had an extreme, vital, and *physical* importance for me. Reading her books provoked a keen distress that stunned me to the point of anguish and pain; it dislodged me, moved me toward another, corporeal, space that seemed to me in the end a woman's space. Meeting with Marguerite Duras completely overwhelmed me. I could hardly stand the tension of the first interview, faced with her gaze. It was unfortunate, in any event, that this tape had to be reduced to a few lines in *Le Monde*'s profile (which, as we understood afterward, would not be accepted). Many of the questions that nagged at us and fascinated us, that put so much into play inside us, had only been touched upon. (I say "we," for it's obvious that Marguerite Duras asks me at least as many questions as I ask her and that I'm as implicated in all of this as she is.) So we thought about continuing our talks. Marguerite Duras suggested that I come to her country house. I stayed there nearly the whole summer, captivated by the charm of that house—where she filmed *Nathalie Granger*—by the color, odor, taste almost of the thick walls and faded floral fabrics that make that house a privileged place, a childhood dream. I was captivated by Marguerite Duras's generosity and openness; by this anxious, ardent, tormented, peremptory, and and intransigent woman. Perhaps you will be able to sense something of the unique atmosphere in which our conversations took place and of the friendship that grew between us.

And, between the recordings of our interviews, we made jam . . .

Xavière Gauthier

First Interview

X.G. *How can one begin?*

M.D. What should I say now?

X.G. *Well, let's say something about how language is organized in your texts. It's probably very different from the way it's organized in texts by men.*

M.D. I'm never concerned about the sense or the meaning. If there's sense, it shows up afterward. Anyway, it's never a concern.

X.G. *Actually, I wasn't talking about sense. How is it that language gets arranged in the book, on paper?*

M.D. The word counts more than the syntax. More than anything, it's words—without articles—that come and impose themselves. The grammatical tense follows, at a distance.

X.G. *I was thinking . . . without articles. In L'Amour—we'll begin at the end—there's a moment when you say: "Isn't aware of being looked at." There's not even a personal pronoun, which would be "she"; then, "isn't aware of" is negative, and "being looked at" is passive. I was wondering if this isn't a sort of retreat, a return to standard grammatical meaning.*

M.D. She's not conscious of herself. So blanks turn up, you see. It happens like this—I'll try to explain: perhaps the blanks appear as a result of a violent rejection of syntax. Yes, I think that's it; that sounds right.

X.G. *And when you say "blanks," is that the same as emptiness or gaps?*

1

M.D.   Someone has said the word anesthesia—suppressions.

X.G.   *I was wondering whether this blank itself wouldn't be something of woman, truly of woman. If there is, for example, a grammatical chain, where there's a space in it, wouldn't that space be where woman would be?*

M.D.   Who knows?

X.G.   *Well, because that would be a rupture of the symbolic chain. And in your books, there is just that. To me, that's very clear. I don't know if it's blank. For me, it would be a little like holding your breath. You're in a rhythm, and then there are moments when you can no longer breathe, when something's blocked.*

M.D.   I know that the place where this writes itself, where I write it— when I do—is a place where breathing is shortened and there's a drop in sensory perception. Not everything is heard, only certain things, you see. This is a black and white place. If there is color, it gets added on. And the color is not immediate; it's not realistic.

X.G.   L'Amour *is in black and white, like the positive and negative of a film . . .*

M.G.   Yes, or like writing . . .

X.G.   *. . . with just some touches, I think, of blue, particularly blue eyes. We'd have to see at what moments this recurs. It's really quite seldom, a small shading.*

M.D.   In *Abhan, Sabana, David*, there are blue eyes. You can't look at blue eyes. They can't be taken up in a gaze. You travel *through* blue eyes. You look at dark eyes. The darkness stops the gaze. It offers resistance. Blue eyes don't. Blue has no gaze. Just holes. I think I say at a certain point: "the holes" . . . and you see, I had to write a lot of books to get to this point. There's a whole period—up to *Moderato cantabile*—during which I wrote books that I don't recognize.

X.G.   *Weren't these books fuller because of that? Because in them, the place for a hole or a blank was missing. I don't know, I'm thinking of* Le Marin de Gibraltar; *is that what you mean by first books?*

M.D.   Yes, *Le Marin de Gibraltar* or *Le Barrage*.

2

X.G. *I would see these as more masculine books.*

M.D. Yes, perhaps. That could be.

X.G. *Where there's not a place for a blank yet, where the space still isn't—I don't know—large enough or silent enough.*

M.D. But how is it that . . . I mean, do you think that you'd have to write a lot of books before, before writing, say, *Détruire?* that someone couldn't begin with *Détruire?*

X.G. *You know, Freud said that woman, to become a woman, has to change sex. That is, she's a boy first, and then at the moment she becomes a woman, she changes sex. I wonder whether this doesn't happen to all women—whether maybe some never really make the change for that matter. When you do make it, it has to be after a certain amount of time when you have been just a man; that is, when you're . . .*

M.D. . . . in a state of complete, instilled alienation, you mean.

X.G. *And what you were saying a while ago, that your mother would have liked for you to be a boy, and so in the beginning you tried to fulfill this desire. To really be a boy, that is, to take your place in the world of boys. Wasn't it something like that?*

M.D. Maybe so. But no psychiatrist has spoken to me about it, in any case.

X.G. *Were they men, the psychiatrists?*

M.D. Yes. But it's a fact that with the other books I was—and it's still important and interesting to say so, I think—I was going to work every day. I wrote the way people go to the office, every day, peacefully; I would take a couple of months to do a book, and then all at once this changed. With *Moderato,* it wasn't as calm. And then after May 1968, with *Détruire,* it wasn't like that at all anymore. That is, the book was written in several days, and that made me really frightened for the first time. Yes, it really began with *Le Ravissement de Lol. V. Stein.* At that time I was coming out of treatment for alcoholism, so I don't know whether this fright—I've thought about it a lot and I've never managed to figure it out— whether this fright that I knew while writing it wasn't also the fear

3

of being without alcohol; whether it wasn't the aftereffect of detoxification. I can't tell.

X.G.   *Well, maybe that played a role, but it wasn't just that.*

M.D.   The fear began with *Lol. V. Stein* and a little with *Moderato*, I have to say. It became extreme with *Détruire*, almost dangerous.

X.G.   *Isn't it with* Le Ravissement *that there begins to be the hole?*

M.D.   The experience of it, then the experimentation. That goes back to what you were saying: I was experimenting with this blank in the chain.

X.G.   *It happens through forgetfulness at first, and forgetfulness is also a blank. It seems to be based—if you can talk about a base, because that's really not the word—in* Le Ravissement *on the forgetfulness of suffering.*

M.D.   It's more of an omission.

X.G.   *Yes, an omission. Perhaps that's what's really frightening, because you begin to enter the lack.*

M.D.   In *Lol. V. Stein?*

X.G.   *From* Lol. V. Stein *on. I know that when I read your books, it puts me into a state that's very . . . very powerful and I get quite uncomfortable. It's very hard to speak or do anything after reading them. I don't know whether it's fear, but it's truly a dangerous state to get into, for me.*

M.D.   So we're talking about the same state that makes . . . when they're written or read . . . I would really like to know how you can get to the . . . at least how you can circumscribe it.

X.G.   *Circumscribe it, name it.*

M.D.   When I tell you that this or that is a perimeter . . . without sleep . . . you see . . . I can't get anywhere.

X.G.   *But does one get anywhere? In your books, no one gets anywhere, that's just it. There's also the question of movement, I think. Movements are always quite imperceptible, sliding, in a way, and that's not at all the same as advancing. I mean, there's no advancement, or if there is, it's circular.*

M.D.   Yes, that's what it is, that's pretty good. Nothing advances. Nothing

4

goes anywhere, but things move.

X.G. *Things move, and slide. And maybe that's it as well—this space that is developing and is, I think, so particular to you—a thick space as well. I see it as thickness; maybe that's why the pace is slow or restrained. There's this great thickness—which is closed, but at the same time you know there's an outside.*

M.D. Yes, but does the outside put a pressure on this place?

X.G. *Yes. It's the outside that closes the space in on itself.*

M.D. Yes, but it's not present at all when I'm writing.

X.G. *Ah, yes it is.*

M.D. Well, I forget about it. I get inside somewhere, and it closes itself off.

X.G. *Completely?*

M.D. Yes. But that's not where it's dangerous; it's when you're trying to get out you see.

X.G. *When you're trying to get to the outside again?*

M.D. Yes.

X.G. *And it's not even present as a threat when you're on the inside? It doesn't exist anymore?*

M.D. No. On the inside there's an extraordinary surveillance so that nothing escapes. But what it's about is simply noticing . . . the accidents: that is, a displacement, a voice.

X.G. *Yes, the voice too. The voice is extremely important in your books.*

M.D. They're public voices, voices that don't address each other. Just as they don't move, they don't address one another.

X.G. *Do they even come from the person, these voices?*

M.D. Maybe not.

X.G. *Don't they just travel through it?*

M.D. Yes, they do. Just as the book travels through—it's the same movement. Yes, that's it.

X.G. *So it passes through the subject. I think there's the question of the subject in your books also. I mean, that it's completely called into question. The traditional Cartesian subject that's completely whole, opaque, and round; it is utterly punctured . . .*

M.D. Cracked open, you mean?

5

x.g.   *Yes.*

m.d.   But people do read for that, and one needs to be aware of it. I'm moving into another domain here. Because when I began not being able to avoid that kind of book, so to speak—I can't talk about it any other way—and no longer trying to avoid them, I thought no one would read them. You see how dangerous it is, tremendously so; it's lunatic. But then there turned out to be readers . . . even men . . .

x.g.   *Did that seem strange to you?*

m.d.   Yes.

x.g.   *And what did the men tell you?*

m.d.   The word "sick" appeared in every letter.

x.g.   *Sick?*

m.d.   "Reading your books has made me sick."

x.g.   *But this didn't happen to women?*

m.d.   Women too.

x.g.   *In the same way?*

m.d.   Yes. But taking this a bit further, we could say: these books are painful, to write and to read, and this pain should lead us toward a place . . . a place of experimentation. What I mean is that they're painful, painful because they're works that move toward an area that's not hollowed out yet, maybe.

x.g.   *Not brought to light yet.*

m.d.   This is the blank in the chain you were talking about. I don't mean in psychoanalytic terms . . . I mean something about what is feminine, you know?

x.g.   *Yes, yes.*

m.d.   Maybe that's what causes the pain.

x.g.   *Yes, I think so. And maybe this hasn't come out yet; no one's put a finger on it. Maybe the fact of showing the blank,[2] showing the hole, makes people sick, and for good reason. In this sense, it's totally subversive.*

m.d.   Do *you* think that *Détruire* and *L'Amour* . . . that a man couldn't write these?

x.g.   *I'm convinced of it. I'm convinced that it can only be a woman,*

6

and really a woman. The difficulty is to show why exactly. But it's
clear when I read them . . . I mean, you told me that your first
name isn't on your books anymore; that from time to time only
"Duras" appears. It would be interesting to know whether some
people—assuming there are *people who don't know you—might*
think you're a man. Because I can't imagine. Has anyone ever
written to you, who didn't know—people who thought they were
writing to a man?

M.D.   No, people know who I am. But why does only Duras appear now?
       I've been told it was asexual.

X.G.   *Asexual! What you write?*

M.D.   Yes.

X.G.   *I don't think so at all. There's an eroticism . . .*

M.D.   Yes, but a kind of eroticism . . .

X.G.   *. . . that could be from a man or woman?*

M.D.   It's mutual, yes.

X.G.   *No, I don't think so at all. I don't think that it can be from anyone*
       but a woman, but it's hard to explain. Because there is no mutual
       eroticism. What I mean is that . . . the body is different, so . . . so
       what it feels is different too, by definition.

M.D.   You're probably right.

X.G.   *Could a man, in his sexuality, show the blank this way? Because it's*
       sexual, too, this blank, this emptiness.

M.D.   No, I don't think so; he would interfere. I don't interfere.

X.G.   *Well, there you are.*

M.D.   Basically, what I do . . . what happens to me is maybe just . . . that:
       an experience that I let happen . . . do you think so? Maybe it's
       just . . . really, just . . .

X.G.   *Right, it's not so simple. An experience that you listen to . . .*

M.D.   Yes . . . one that takes effect.

X.G.   *Yes . . . one that you let take effect inside you . . . at the risk of . . .*
       of insane anguish.

M.D.   Yes. It's always hard to talk about that, because . . . you know, you're
       always afraid that people will misunderstand. I mean, if you're going

7

to let yourself be carried away like that, it's better to get rid of the fear of madness. So, then, I must have tried, which meant that . . . madness was no longer the bogeyman that they—that men—had erected in front of me all my life.

X.G. *It's men who erected this bogeyman?*

M.D. Yes.

X.G. *And Lol. V. Stein, for example, the character of Lol. V. Stein—is that what happens to her?*

M.D. What happens is that she becomes . . . there's a continual corrective in her life, isn't there? She does everything as if it were possible; she was taught to speak, to walk, to get married, to make love, to have children, and everything happens . . . I think a lot of women are like that. You know, all of a sudden, that's what I think: they do their job as it is dictated by men. But for her, for Lol. V. Stein, things were easier because, in the beginning, the absence of pain— or rather, her failed attempt to join with the love between Anne-Marie Stretter and Richardson. She failed completely; that is, there's a missing link there, too. The jealousy wasn't lived out, the pain wasn't lived out. The link was broken, so that everything that follows in the chain is false. It's at another level.

X.G. *And it's exactly that level that's interesting.*

M.D. Yes, but there had to be an accident.

X.G. *Yes. In* Détruire, *for example, the accident would be the dead child, for Elisabeth Alione?*

M.D. For Elisabeth Alione, it's the dead child.

X.G. *I think that's really important too. Definitely. Since a woman, in principle, has a reproductive system, not a productive system. Reproductive—that is, having children. The fact that it all begins with the failure of reproduction, that is, the dead child . . . maybe it's from that point on that that other space can be opened up.*

M.D. Maybe. It's happened to me . . . but in *Détruire* it's Alissa, the newcomer. The ground is the dead child, but what walks upon the ground is Alissa. She comes along—and Stein.

8

X.G.   *But maybe it's the child's death that permits their coming.*

M.D.   Ah, yes.

X.G.   *So what about Alissa and Elisabeth's relationship?*

M.D.   She shows up on the scene and she chats; she begins by asking questions, Alissa, right? nothing but questions. She is utter destruction, Alissa is, negation. She leaves the book and Elisabeth Alione . . . stripped. *Détruire* is like a preface . . .

X.G.   *She's stripped of her social persona too, isn't she, as Bernard Alione's wife?*

M.D.   Yes, that starts to happen. That begins after leaving the hotel—that is, after the end of the book. Stein doesn't act. It's through the mediation of Elisabeth Alione . . . no, of Alissa, that he acts. He doesn't have any relationship with Elisabeth Alione, ever.

X.G.   *But on the other hand, he acts upon Max Thor.*

M.D.   Yes.

X.G.   *You were saying the other day that . . . that Alissa was androgynous, somewhat.*

M.D.   In fact, I nearly had Stein played by Tatiana Moukhine. And some of the young men asked me if they could play Alissa.

X.G.   *Would you have liked that?*

M.D.   It was an interesting idea. I mean, it was . . .

X.G.   *But still, isn't it necessary for the "masculine" role that Alissa plays to come from a woman? If it were played straight by a man, wouldn't it lose something?*

M.D.   Yes, it would lose the listening faculty, in any event . . . [*Interruption.*]

X.G.   *. . . Alissa could work because she was a woman, and if she had been a man, it wouldn't have been the same.*

M.D.   You really think it wouldn't have been the same?

X.G.   *Yes, I do.*

M.D.   Right, with Alissa it's a question of malleability. She can be molded.

X.G.   *Yes, she can be molded, but at the same time, she's the one who leads the dance of desire.*

9

M.D. Oh, completely. Stein can't do *that*.

X.G. *No, but he still has a very important role. And yet I can't place him very well.*

M.D. Perhaps he has a nominal role, actually. Since Alissa's initial shock, if you remember, has to do with the name of Stein. That's even another . . .

X.G. *Yes. That's really quite a problem, the name.*

M.D. Stein . . . and she is already in a certain state of transgression.

X.G. *Yes, and what about the name of Lol. V. Stein?*

M.D. The same.

X.G. *It's the same for Lol period, V period. That's always seemed incredible to me. That break, and you never know, you will never know what comes after it. Another blank maybe?*

M.D. Ah, but she's named in the book: Lola Valérie Stein.

X.G. *That's true, we learn it, but regardless, what her real name is is Lol. V. Stein, right?*

M.D. It's her real name because she gives it to herself. After her illness, she names herself . . . and for good.[3]

X.G. *Women don't have names, by definition.*

M.D. Right. We could talk about where we get the horror for our names.

X.G. *Yes, the problem's with last names, the name of the father. The father being what determines the symbolic order and the law. To the extent that one doesn't want to bow down to the law,[4] maybe we have to do something about the name of the father, maybe even do away with it . . . anyway, there's a problem with it.*

M.D. Many, many women are horrified by their names. Even women who don't write.

X.G. *Can one write while keeping one's father's name?*

M.D. That's something that never seemed to me . . . that never seemed possible for a second. But I've never tried to find out why I've been so horrified by my name that I can hardly manage to pronounce it. I never had a father.

X.G. *You never had a father? But . . .*

M.D. Well, I had him only for a short while . . . which was long enough.

X.G.   *He must have made himself felt through his absence, didn't he?*

M.D.   Of course.

X.G.   *Because even now, I think that in a family . . . a woman who doesn't have a man around, that's a problem; the children must feel it.*

M.D.   But this isolation that certain women keep themselves in, this isolation from men, might be necessary.

X.G.   *What do you mean? Who are you thinking of?*

M.D.   Of some groups of women I know who live very far apart from men, very separate, who don't want even the least contact anymore. Do you think one has to reach that point?

X.G.   *I don't know.*

M.D.   It's a problem.

X.G.   *It's definitely a problem. I think it's interesting that such a thing exists—that there are women, and especially groups of women, who try to exist by themselves, actually without men. Because we get so many things from men to start out with. We get—I mean they impose on us . . . so many things in the game come to us from men that it might be necessary to cut ourselves off.*

M.D.   But a real society of women is being created.

X.G.   *That's important because historically it's never existed.*

M.D.   I know some women personally who want only female interactions, who are comfortable only in female relationships.

X.G.   *Yes, they often live together in their own community. They say that their bodies have always been mutilated and assaulted by men in every way, either physically or through advertising or whatever, and that now they need time to find themselves: that is, to find themselves among one another, just to begin to live their bodies, to discover them, touch them, feel them. They could be right; I don't know.*

M.D.   They don't live any masculine experience with a man anymore?

X.G.   *A lot of them don't.*

M.D.   Yes, I have friends like that.

X.G.   *Many have stopped all interactions with men.*

M.D. But what about, as is often the case, when desire has been lived through the man?

X.G. *Exactly—it's true that even women's desire, for two women together, often passes through men, still.*

M.D. That's quite true.

X.G. *But it seems to me that often there's a decrease in desire. Maybe it's temporary. One must hope that it's temporary.*

M.D. Between women, you mean?

X.G. *Yes. Meaning that they're a little lost and that—I don't know— there's a drop in libido; I'm not sure what to call it. Maybe even now when there's not that support anymore, desire circulates less.*

M.D. Yes, it's difficult; it's almost unimaginable. It's like living a mutilation, isn't it?

X.G. *Yes, but is it that way because that's how it is, or simply because we've gotten used to a certain kind of society?*

M.D. That's how it is: desire has been lived with men until now. That's all.

X.G. *Now, today, family structure is with a man, usually with the father. What's interesting, I think, as an experiment, is that sometimes the women have children—I mean, they had children before—and since they don't see men anymore, they live and raise their children together. Consequently, these children don't see anyone but women until they're school age. I'd really like to know how this affects them. Children with mothers, with several mothers.*

M.D. Do you think . . . finally, that . . . several mothers . . .

X.G. *They certainly know that one is their mother. But in the father's place, there are other women.*

M.D. Men, on the other hand, are in a state of total incomprehension.

X.G. *About that?*

M.D. Yes, they don't have the capacity to understand it.

X.G. *It frightens them because obviously it puts them in danger.*

M.D. It's sort of the end of the world, what's being described here, what we're saying, isn't it?

X.G. *The end of the world or the beginning of another story. Because until now there is an entire history of a society just of men. I don't know . . . for example, I'm thinking along these lines: the fact that men do military service, nearly all of them do. They live a life among men; even if it's imposed, they live it.*

M.D.   But the male community never ends, even after the service.

X.G.   *Right, but I mean that that's where it's the easiest to see, and that it marks them as well. But it's true that the male community never ends. That's why it's interesting that there are small groups of women trying to make female communities or communes.*

M.D.   I've lived a lot with men, only with men, and I realize that gradually I've been changing.

X.G.   *Really?*

M.D.   And that I find myself more and more with women.

X.G.   *And do you think that your books have something to do with this?*

M.D.   My books?

X.G.   *Yes.*

M.D.   Yes, but also homosexuals, I'd say.

X.G.   *Yes, exactly. Maybe it's important to introduce the problem of women's relationship to male homosexuality.*

M.D.   Yes.

X.G.   *I don't know how or why, but it seems to me that women often . . .*

M.D.   We're talking about two transgressions that run into each other, aren't we?

X.G.   *The transgression of the woman . . .*

M.D.   . . . and of the homosexual.

X.G.   *Yes.*

M.D.   Male.[5]

X.G.   *Yes. Often women who have transgressed against something, by being productive, do in fact enjoy being in the company of male homosexuals.*

M.D.   Yes. I think, of course, that homosexuality, as something natural, doesn't exist.

X.G.   *No.*

M.D.   I think that it's a transgression . . . of a different order.

X.G.   *A social order?*

M.D. Yes. And it is as such that the transgressions join each other, that they join the others, if you like.

X.G. *Yes.*

M.D. At the start of male homosexuality there is always an accident that makes the man break off from the path of heterosexuality, isn't there?

X.G. *And do you think that for women it's the same? To the extent that they transgressed against something, there was an accident?*

M.D. Yes.

X.G. *What would it be?*

M.D. Only, in male homosexuality, the accident is a childhood trauma, that's certain. In the case of the woman, it can take place much later. In adulthood.

X.G. *Yes.*

M.D. You see women do a complete turnaround at thirty or forty or twenty-five, but you never see a man do a turnaround in the same way.

X.G. *No. Why not? Would this be a triumph for the woman?*

M.D. This change?

X.G. *Yes.*

M.D. It proves something on her terrain. About her terrain. It proves quite simply that she's not as profoundly alienated as she thinks.

X.G. *Yes, but what is woman's terrain? Isn't that just what's so difficult to find? She certainly has to have one of her own . . . but . . . does society leave us the room?*

M.D. Society has . . . is more and more frightened by woman—and with good reason. I don't see anything in the history of progress—really, that is, in the history of freedom—nothing that has happened as quickly as the women's liberation movement. In the nineteenth century, the idea of revolution took ten times longer, fifty times longer.

X.G. *But why, do you think?*

M.D. It's taken off. Nothing can stop it anymore. Why? Well, because there was the double union of the progress of the revolutionary ideal, wasn't there, which already presented an entire . . . like a . . . a procedure, a machine to unalienate, as it were, that was in our reach, right? The inclination to analyze, our inclination to analyze comes from that. I don't know whether it's right or wrong, but . . . above all, it's Marxist, don't you think?

X.G. *Yes.*

M.D. So, that means that a whole step was skipped, that had been taken before. And then—all right, probably it's that . . . other joint efforts were grafted onto this, young people's movements from all over the world, a liberation of man, of the young man, which produced the hippie, for example, that vacant being who already presented himself almost as a model of the androgyne.[6] You know, like the antihero, which meant that all of a sudden, for the woman, there was a hole, an emptiness to fill, and how come we hadn't thought of it before? That's the mystery. Because I think . . . I'm not very familiar with the issue, but it seems that liberation movements before World War II were false liberation movements, weren't they? Don't you think so?

X.G. *Women's movements?*

M.D. Yes.

X.G. *Suffragette movements? Yes, absolutely. That is, I think that those movements were completely idealistic, quite simply, not taking Marxist criticism into account.*

M.D. Right.

X.G. *They weren't materialist. It's only now that this is taking place.*

M.D. How do we account for that? Let's take another example. Isn't there . . . (I've already said this, but in England—well it doesn't matter) 80 or 90 percent of the European proletariat is Marxist; I don't think there's one worker in ten who doesn't know the law . . . no, out of ten workers, nine definitely know the law of surplus value. Fine, but that knowledge isn't enough to prompt political action. Something else has to enter into it.

X.G. *What's that?*

M.D. I'm thinking of current revolutionary research, the accident that

15

would make a man enter the political struggle; the man armed with this knowledge would move into action. We haven't found it yet. But I think that for the woman this knowledge is already . . . it works differently; that is, this knowledge translates itself immediately because it's possibly the first knowledge she has.

X.G. *Yes . . .*

M.D. In man's case, it comes after an infinity of other kinds of knowledge . . . practices: whereas, for woman, it's the first knowledge that belongs to her.

X.G. *It's not a knowledge—I don't know, I'm just talking off the top of my head—isn't it a knowledge that's more organic, closer to the body?*

M.D. Yes, but I call that knowledge . . . how do we name it? . . . Yes, maybe woman gets it corporeally—yes, corporeally, quite simply. A proletarian who's informed, informed of his alienation, is politicized, but he's not political yet. Whereas a woman who's armed, a woman who . . . who . . . is informed of her alienation is already political.

X.G. *Yes.*

M.D. That's why it all goes so fast. Do you agree?

X.G. *Yes, yes. I understand, yes. But what I was wondering is whether . . . all right, the woman, by giving out this first knowledge, this first—I don't know—information, wasn't she running the risk, at that point, of getting taken over again by the man, who says it or writes it or . . . because, even so, that's his domain.*

M.D. The risk of being translated, you mean?

X.G. *Yes.*

M.D. That's the greatest danger we face. Speak about women to men, and they'll all tell you: "In our opinion, woman . . . and so forth." We laugh. And they don't understand why we're laughing. I think that every woman should conduct an experiment around her; the extent to which man is alienated is astounding. And we've lived alongside that for a very long time without seeing it.

X.G. *Without seeing it, without saying it; it's beginning to get said now.*

M.D. Without saying it. But it's truly astounding. [*Silence.*] The other day,

I took part in a conversation about . . . it was . . . what was said was very simple, that now a woman can begin to travel alone in relative peace, in trains, hotels, streets. We were talking about Italy—everyone's spent abominable vacations in Italy, alone, right? Well, there were several women and a man there, and we were talking about this, and you know what the man linked it up with? Don Juanism! [*Laughter.*] We were talking about women who had been subjected to this, who were no longer experiencing it, and who would no longer accept being subjected to it. And the man got the topic wrong; he thought we were talking about Don Juanism. You see people who are for women's liberation, leftists, anarchists, whatever . . . who say to you: "I love women, I adore women!" And I say: "Just like cars?" [*Laughter.*]

X.G. *Yes, that makes me think of imperialists who talk about the people they colonize by saying, "But we like them a lot." And the thing is that they're really sincere: "We really like them." "Me, I love women" always makes me think of that.*

M.D. "I adore," even. Along with the . . . the "What can I tell you? I love women, that's just how I am—I can't get along without them!"

X.G. *Oh, exactly, just like they can't get along without cars.*

M.D. Yes. [*Silence.*] All right, you can try to enlighten them, but when you do it violently, the man goes through real pain.

X.G. *Yes, a man can't accept it. They don't like to hear what they are.*[7]

M.D. And then you think . . . this is a blind spot, we're confronting an opacity, here, a total blindness; they don't *see.*

X.G. *That's it, but they're not interested in seeing. I mean that this calls so much into question what a man's always been, and also what he's been throughout literature. It all starts to crumble then.*

M.D. Yes, everything crumbles for him. [*Silence.*] But don't you think that they all live with a nostalgia for violence? For muscle?

X.G. *Absolutely.*

M.D. There's a marine in every man. Some dare to speak of a nostalgia for war, but I see that as a generally unconfessed nostalgia, don't you? There's the family marine, the wife's marine, the child's marine, papa-marine [*laughter*], but they're all marines; I believe that every man is much more like a general, a military man, than like the least woman.

X.G. *That's really good, what you're saying. I really like it because that's so much the way it is.*

M.D. It's the phallic class; it's a class phenomenon. That really has to be said.

X.G. *Yes.*

M.D. I'm not accusing them now.

X.G. *No, it's an analysis. I don't think there's any need to be aggressive either.*

M.D. We have to wait for it to pass, I mean, we have to wait until entire generations of men disappear.

X.G. *There's still a lot of work to be done with women; I mean, there's a lot of work toward recognition among women, isn't there? Because men have divided them so much.*

M.D. Well . . . yes. There's a jealousy between men that doesn't exist among women, don't you think?

X.G. *I would really like for it to be that way, but I don't know. I believe anyway that at the moment women are very much at odds, very divided among themselves. I wish there were a collusion, a complicity . . . maybe that's there too, but around men there's a rivalry, a possessiveness in women, isn't there?*

M.D. When a woman . . . I've just discovered a woman painter, a great woman painter who's name is Socquet, and discovering her was a true joy. It's something I feel implicated in.

X.G. *Yes. I can really understand that because I also feel implicated when there's . . .*

M.D. When Sarraute had such success with her play, with her play *Isma*, I felt a real joy. And then, telling about it to my friends, I noticed that this joy was felt by women.

X.G. *Ah, yes.*

M.D. We aren't in competition because we're the opposition.

X.G.   *Yes. Anyway, that's how it should be.*

M.D.   It's men who control the market. So obviously, in that business, they're competitors, but as for us? [*Silence.*] We could talk about criticism, if you like.

X.G.   *Ah yes, masculine criticism. Criticism is masculine.*

M.D.   Yes. [*Silence.*] What's to be said about it? We could maybe talk about it a bit?

X.G.   *I don't know. What have critics, men, said about your books, for example?*

M.D.   They say very little, you know.

X.G.   *That means something in itself.*

M.D.   Yes, I live on my foreign royalties. Right now, I'm living on my English royalties; two years ago I lived on my German royalties. In France, it's nearly a total blackout.

X.G.   *But why?*

M.D.   I don't know.

X.G.   *That's quite odd, when everyone knows you and everyone recognizes you as a writer. So what's going on? Is there a conspiracy of silence? Do people really accept a woman writer?*

M.D.   Or is it rather that we're obliged to be clandestine? I don't know. In France I consider myself to be prohibited.

X.G.   *And does that have to do with the fact, among others, that you're a woman?*

M.D.   Oh yes. Though to what extent, I couldn't say.

X.G.   *But it comes into play?*

M.D.   Wouldn't you think so?

X.G.   *Oh yes, I do. I certainly do. I remember personally having had an article in* Les Lettres françaises, *and a man said—I don't remember the exact words, but it was something of this sort—"Well, well, well, isn't this amusing, a woman who writes!" Really. That's pretty amazing, isn't it?*

M.D.   Yes.

X.G.   *And he acted very concerned about it all . . .*

M.D. Don't you think that the first women who wrote played the role of *enfants terribles* in literature? They played the clown in order to amuse men.

X.G. *Yes, yes.*

M.D. Colette did that.

X.G. *Yes, it was only at that . . .*

M.D. That was the price.

X.G. *Yes . . . it was only at that price that they could be accepted.*

M.D. Yes.

X.G. *All right. But to the extent that they don't do this anymore, they aren't allowed to . . . to pass finally.*

M.D. What we're going to come to is that men are going to get even in another way. Women's literature is going to form this terrain from which point . . . this terrain, this terrain of the novel, because women are still in the novel for the most part—I'm not speaking for myself because I don't feel that I do novels. Anyway, that's what I see being published in abundance, and men are going to practice their theoretical imbecility upon them. I mean, there'll be a co-opting on that basis. A man is most reassured when a woman with six kids in low-cost housing doesn't do anything but talk about that, about her low-cost housing and her six kids.

X.G. *Furthermore, that's why he gave her six kids.*

M.D. Right.

X.G. *It's not done for nothing.*

M.D. So, reassured, the man takes this woman's book and begins to legislate. Which is to say, she's done nothing but add to a literature, a literature that serves her as compost. If she doesn't talk about these low-cost housing units, about living in low-cost housing and about her six kids, he plays the cop. He censors. Who does she think she is?

X.G. *Right.*

M.D. Quite a few men have written about me saying, "Oh, we liked it so much better when she was simple!"

X.G. *Is that true?*

M.D. Yes.

X.G. *But that's just it. I really think that your books are dangerous for men.*

M.D. As far as that goes, a poll was taken, and . . . my readers are young people.

X.G. *Men and women?*

M.D. Yes—well, the poll didn't account for the sex.

X.G. *But your readers are young people for the most part?*

M.D. Yes. I do have older readers, but they stick to my first books.

X.G. *Ah, yes. No, you really have to have something special if you're going to take the risks of passing and still get to where you are. Not everybody can have this talent.*[8] *[Silence.]*

M.D. When you write a woman's book, you see really well; I find that people do a double reading: they read really well what she thought herself obliged to say as a woman. In poetry, the transgression is simpler, more immediate. In the novel . . .

X.G. *The transgression is simpler in poetry? That's funny. It's harder for me to imagine a women's poetry.*

M.D. But that's what they started with when they began to write.

X.G. *Exactly, there's a whole realm that they reserve ever so nicely for women, the realm of flowers, I mean . . .*

M.D. Of *fioretti?*

X.G. *Yes. Because then when people say women's literature, there's this idea of flowers, and maternity; there's a whole . . .*

M.D. Nature.

X.G. *Nature, of course! And that writing, finally, is a man's writing; that is, the image that those women make for themselves is a man's image, isn't it?*

M.D. Yes, of course, what else would you expect? The maidservant who goes out dancing disguises herself as a middle-class woman. The woman who writes disguises herself as . . . as a man.

X.G. *Yes, that is, she thinks that in order to have access to literature, she has to become a man.*

M.D. Yes, it always begins by this aping. That's the first work to be done.

X.G. *To recognize oneself as a woman?*

M.D. Yes, and I didn't escape. When I was twenty and people told me, "It's almost like a man's," I was flattered.

X.G. *Of course you were.*
[*Interruption. Tape erased.*]

X.G. *. . . so you don't believe that there is real strength in woman?*

M.D. Oh, I'm absolutely certain there is. Man is not strong; he's turbulent.

X.G. *That's right. I totally agree with you. That's why he wants to be a marine, because he's not strong. A woman doesn't need that. And I believe there's a strength in female desire, in female sexuality, an immense strength, that man doesn't particularly want to know. And that's what's in your books. At least I experience them that way. In your books, there's the force of female desire, and it's not so pleasant, I suppose, for men—for men who consider themselves men. Anyway, I see it as a calm force, silent, all the stronger because it's silent and calm. It's . . . I don't know how to say it; I was going to say muted, in halftones. But that's absurd because that's still feminine in the way the flower is, and it's not that, it's . . . subterranean, a little bit underground, that is, not a protesting power not a power . . .*

M.D. But one that's potential?

X.G. *Yes.*

M.D. Maybe potential more than anything else.

X.g. *Potential . . . um, well, it's there, it's realized, in a way. Potential would mean not yet realized. It is realized, but it's . . .*

M.D. Are you talking about my books or about life? [*Laughter.*]

X.G. *I was talking about your books. The women's power that appears in your books. In your books it's there. In life it would be potential.*

M.D. But it's not satisfying in my books.

X.G. *No, not at all.*

M.D. But maybe man's weakness is precisely the fact that he is so easily satisfied.

X.G.   *Yes . . . yes. And that's another reason why I think that you can't not know that it's a woman who writes your books, because there's none of this . . . model of male sexuality, with arousal, satisfaction, then it's done and starts over. It's not that way for a woman, and in your books men must be lost because there's always a very forceful tension that is never satisfied.*

M.D.   In the man, you mean?

X.G.   *No, in your books. There's an erotic tension that can never be satisfied.*

M.D.   Yes . . .

X.G.   *So it seems to me, anyway; that's how I feel it.*

M.D.   One can say anything, you know, you can take whatever you want from it. However, I've had a life . . . a sex life . . . real—how do you say this politely? [*Laughter.*] Well, let's say plentiful. And . . . quite violent. With men.

X.G.   *Yes. And why do you say "however"?*

M.D.   Because this sort of claim, if you like, for . . . for contents that never overflow . . . yes, it could seem like a . . . desire—well, desire, let's not use the word "desire"; let's give it it's full range—like a failing in a life, a failing . . .

X.G.   *Yes. But I didn't see it like that.*

M.D.   You don't see the link?

X.G.   *No.*

M.D.   Yes, well I see this a little academically.

X.G.   *I wasn't thinking of it at all in the sense of failing. I was thinking in the sense of a force that doesn't run out, not one that never gets satisfied. When I say that she doesn't find satisfaction, I don't mean it's unfortunate that the woman doesn't get satisfied. I mean that she can't be satisfied.*

M.D.   Yes, that's part of what defines her.

X.G.   *Because she has this power, because she has this force . . .*

M.D.   That's right. Oh yes.

X.G.   *. . . that always makes her live. But I find that what you tell me* *about your life fits really well with this; I mean that* you *live a sexual life, but there are very few women, finally, I think, even now, who . . .*

M.D.   But I think that women don't live a sexual life because you can't ask women to . . . not to go . . . not to mix with anyone but women—right?—but I think that they don't live it because they still have a medieval fear of infidelity.[9] That's another thing they have to get over. Plural experience could get you over it.

X.G.   *Yes. That's definitely true. I think that they're still very much enclosed in . . .*

M.D.   Ah, yes. It's completely barbarous.

X.G.   *They need a husband or a lover, it doesn't matter, but a man—their man, that is. And here again, here's another thing that your books sweep aside . . . just like that! What does "possessiveness" or "fidelity" mean to Max Thor, for example, and Alissa? It has no meaning.*

M.D.   No, it doesn't make any sense at all.

X.G.   *That's all swept aside, I think.*

M.D.   And love is lived.

X.G.   *Yes.*

M.D.   And love is lived. What's frightening is that I see lots of young people, and all I see is that love isn't lived. Maybe this moment has to come. It's . . . it's fairly dramatic. Maybe it's a kind of Pascalian bet, they make love . . . they make love, they do it, they do it, a lot. But without . . . without any passion . . . what do you think?

X.G.   *Yes, I was thinking that, waiting for you to say it. I was thinking of the word "passion," and you're right; I think that it's . . . that it might be missing. But maybe it's a phase. Maybe it's the fact that they have more possibilities. It seems to me, anyway, that the sexual field is opening up.*

M.D.   It's so easy. It's simple. All the barriers, mostly, have been . . . for young people.

X.G.   *Yes, for certain young people.*

M.D.   For certain young people, yes, but they're the ones we're talking about.

X.G.   *Yes, they just sort of plunge in, and passion will follow, won't it?*

M.D.   It's still impressive. There's a kind of sexual decoloration . . .

X.G.   *They're a little frightened, too, really.*

M.D.   . . . of no-man's-land.

X.G.   *They talk about it a lot and they're really frightened. The boys as well as the . . . the boys more than the girls, even. I mean frightened of living something, a passion.*

M.D.   Do you think that they avoid it or that it just doesn't happen? That they don't give in to it?

X.G.   *They try not to give in to it.*

M.D.   I've got a twenty-five-year-old son who reproaches his father and me for having lived together for eleven years; he doesn't *know* jealousy. It's a dead word.

       [*Erased tape.*]

       There are instructions for the use of woman that are dictated by man.

       [*Erased tape.*]

       They act—I don't know—as if the women agree.

X.G.   *Yes, when you say, "Women are shared," obviously . . .*

M.D.   When love comes, and it's often in the woman that it arises, it's immediately punished. There's an entire society that lives that way.

X.G.   *Because, even so, women have always played the role of shared object, shared . . . that is, um, object of exchange, object of circulation.*

M.D.   Yes, but if the woman is prostituted—to use a worn-out word, and that's . . . for lack of a better one, let's use it—if the woman is prostituted, *she* has to want it. It shouldn't have to be dictated by men, and that's something like what happens in young people. I know of some tragic cases.

X.G.   *And do you think they have* jouissance, *these women?*

M.D.   I'm convinced that they don't.

x.g.   *That's a question I've asked myself.*

m.d.   Well, now, we're inside . . . within a perimeter where eroticism is completely banished, where there's a misery, an erotic impoverishment, which is exactly the same as the perimeter of our fathers and mothers and grandparents.

x.g.   *That's why it's troubling.*

m.d.   They were raped women. It didn't happen all the time, but 90 percent of the time I think the woman lived in a state of legal rape.

x.g.   *Some women say that rape isn't at all . . . well, that it's also when a woman is raped in a dark alley but that it's almost always in the sexual relationship, and very often they've experienced it as a rape, even when they consented.*

m.d.   They experienced it how?

x.g.   *As a rape.*

m.d.   When the thing is unformulated, is that a rape?

x.g.   *Well, they consider it a rape to the extent that that's how they experience it.*

m.d.   They say that now?

x.g.   *Yes. Maybe it's a rape if the woman doesn't get pleasure. Well, you could say that . . . well . . . that it's really hardly worth it for her to make love if she doesn't get pleasure.*

m.d.   Yes, if the woman gets *jouissance*, it's not a rape anymore, ever, because she wants to make love. [*Silence.*]

x.g.   *And yet . . . yes, it's probably another of the contradictions, that maybe . . . um . . . there's a desire in certain women for rape.*

m.d.   I believed for a long time that frigidity was a myth, a Jesuit story. And, in fact, lots of young women talk to me about it.

x.g.   *But what I think myself, as far as frigidity goes, is that lots of men are frigid. I mean, they have an organic pleasure, fine . . . ejaculation, fine, but that they don't feel . . . they don't have a body. They don't experience the pleasure of the body.*[10]

m.d.   The world of the young people I've been telling you about, which terrorizes me—I don't know whether we should talk about it in the article; I don't think we should, that's something else—but that's exactly it. It happens in thirty seconds, like defecation. This is extremely serious. [*Silence.*] But you can spot a sexually satisfied woman a hundred meters away.

X.G. *Yes!*

M.D. It's true. [*Silence.*] The . . . I think the erotic bond in the couple was frowned upon, has always been frowned upon, hasn't it? [*Inaudible words*] the modern day.

X.G. *How is that?*

M.D. They were looked at askance, a husband and wife who were lovers at the same time, that was frowned upon. It still is. From that standpoint, there's been no progress. You'll tell me we're getting off the subject, but I don't think so.

X.G. *No . . . no . . .*

M.D. I know a couple—among all these young people, a single one—a couple who are still lovers, but the others find this objectionable.

X.G. *Ah, yes. But I still see a lot of very young people who are still very much couples.*

M.D. Don't you think that it's more of an association? It's like a fraternal bond.

X.G. *Maybe so. There is a buddy aspect to it.*

M.D. Yes.

X.G. *There's an overall militancy about it.*

M.G. But you have to admit they have none of the external signs of passion, that sort of burning, that fire, the mortal wound. They don't have that.

X.G. *What you say is frightening. It would mean that . . .*

M.D. Maybe it's a fadeout. The other day, I had a conversation with a friend, a close friend. She said to me: "I'm going to buy a bigger bed; I've got a small bed. For making love, a bigger one's more practical. Do you know where I can get one?" I said to her: "You know, I would never say what you just did. I've done it, but no one ever knew about it. You talk about it the way you'd say "I'm watching a film." She said, "You probably just can't understand." And I said, "You can't understand either." Adultery used to be a . . .

a bogeyman, but really, adultery provides an irreplaceable erotic conditioning.[11]

X.G. *But even with the guilt it could bring along?*

M.D. Well, of course, which also eroticized the relation. Eroticization came from all sides, including fear, physical fear, fear of anger, of violence from the husband, fear of being killed.

X.G. *Yes. We don't run the risk of getting killed anymore these days.*

M.D. No. Except in Africa, in Spain . . .

X.G. *Yes, but at what price?*

M.D. . . . but in the northern part of the Western world . . .

X.G. *But with such an enormous alienation of the woman, don't you think?*

M.D. Yes.

X.G. *That's right. That makes me think of something else, again in your books—I always come back to them. But . . . there's a—this word's not going to fit at all, but anyway, too bad—exhibitionism and voyeurism in them.*

M.D. I see that too.

X.G. *These words don't work at all. I don't know what one should say.*

M.D. There was voyeurism in them, before I found the man, the third person, the intercessor—the man who walks on the beach, for example.

X.G. *Yes, in* L'Amour.

M.D. In *Détruire,* he's the third person.

X.G. *But in* Détruire, *they still leave the window wide and the curtains open.*

M.D. Yes, but Stein is the third man, the witness, the voyeur. But he's official there; he's set up that way.

X.G. *And in* Le Ravissement! *In the field, that's just incredible!*

M.D. Yes. But what is this third person? It's just the one who is informed, the one who arouses, isn't it?

X.G. *Who arouses and who gets* jouissance *too, right?*

M.D. Yes. There's a kind of circulation, so to speak, of *jouissance.*

X.G. *Yes. [Silence.] It's true that in a certain way, you can make love*

28

only in threes. In other words, the third person, even and especially if he isn't there, isn't it necessary for there to be a third so that desire can continue to circulate? Like the triangle in L'Amour, *the triangle that is undone and then re-formed.*

M.D. Yes. I'd really like for us to elucidate that. It's so obscure. I wrote a first novel, a first script. *Détruire* wasn't a first . . . it existed, it was "La Chaise longue." Stein wasn't in it and the book really came into being with Stein, who doesn't make love himself.

X.G. *No, he watches, he knows.*

M.D. He's a kind of parasite, basically. Yes, he watches, he knows.

X.G. *His role is knowing, having a certain kind of knowledge, a familiarity, isn't it?*

M.D. Yes, but probably he knows *jouissance.* Yes. And do you think that this third character—isn't it writing? Do you think you can find it . . . elsewhere?

X.G. *I'm thinking, totally stupidly, of the Oedipal triangle.*

M.D. Which means?

X.G. *Which means the father, mother, and child. If the child desires the mother, the father has to be around—right?—who prohibits but who doesn't just prohibit, who is there and who . . .*

M.D. And who is the rival.

X.G. *Yes, or who complicates things, anyway.*
[Interruption, telephone. Then we look at a text written by Marguerite Duras in a book by Alain Vircondelet: *Marguerite Duras, Ecrivains d'hier et d'aujourd'hui*, published by Seghers.]

M.D. It's not bearable anymore.

X.G. *It's overwhelming.*

M.D. I wanted to take a glance at what I said.

X.G. *Yes, this is quite interesting about women's aptitude for intelligence. I don't know whether we could talk about that.*

M.D. Would you like a glass of wine?

X.G. *Yes, thank you.*
[Interruption.]

M.D. I was talking about this recently; I was asked for interviews almost everywhere—by popular demand no less—even though I don't know how to speak. Writing is different, totally different. Anyway, it's that people realize they're really tired of pure theoretical discourse. This is a woman's discourse because I'm trying . . . this is organic discourse, so to speak, since I don't count on references.

X.G. *That fits in exactly with what you say here in the text[12]—that men are quick to put a heavy theoretical hand on speech that falters.*

M.D. Have you seen the thing on May '68? It's very severe.

X.G. *But it's very good—very, very good; very, very important—and I think when you say that men prevent silence from being heard, and again I come back to your books, it's so rare; in your books silence is heard. There's a place for silence, a big place, isn't there?*

M.D. Yes.

X.G. *And there again, I also believe that only a woman can make silence be heard.*

M.D. Maybe that's why l don't read anymore.

X.G. *Yes, because it's too talkative. And then, right away there's the link you make between women and madmen. Not their assimilation but the way you relate women and madmen; what is that? I'm interested in that. I read a book of poems by a woman called Jacqueline . . . no, Thérèse Plantier. In her preface she began by saying: "If there's a madman, it's certainly woman."*

M.D. Yes, and *I* would say: it's children and women both.

X.G. *Yes, but why?*

M.D. A child less than five is a being who's completely crazy.

X.G. *And a woman?*

M.D. Ah, yes, she's much closer to madness . . . in the way that she's closer to all transgressions.

X.G. *That's what it is. It's like transgression. But what bothers me in the comparison with the child—with the madman, I understand it, but with the child—if there is a transgression, it's completely innocent and completely . . .*

M.D. I'm not comparing; I'm saying they're both crazy, children and women.

X.G.   *Oh, yes.*

M.D.   No, I'm not saying for a second that woman is a child. No, what I say there is—well, I'll read the ending: "'I meet you, I look at you, I speak to you, I leave you.' And then, that's what happens: 'She met him, she looked at him, she spoke to him, she left him.' And then there's a third stage: 'What happened?' And then, the last stage: 'This happened because it's about me.' 'In my internal shadow where the fomenting of myself by myself takes place, in my written region, I *read* that this happened. If I'm a professional, I take up the pen and the piece of paper, and I carry out the conversion of the conversion. What am I doing by doing this? I'm trying to translate the unreadable by using an undifferentiated vehicle, an egalitarian language. So I deprive myself of the internal shadow's integrity which balances, inside me, the life I've lived. I take myself away from the interior mass; I do on the outside what I must do on the inside.' You can say the same thing of woman . . . of man. That, we can say. 'I mutilate myself with the internal shadow, in the best of situations. I have the illusion of creating order when in fact I'm depopulating, of creating light when I'm erasing. Or else you create all light and you're crazy. Madmen carry on *outside* the conversion of the life they live. The illuminating light that penetrates within them has dispelled the internal shadow but replaces it. *Only madmen write completely.*' That's what it is. 'Anybody is more mysterious than a writer.' Any woman is more mysterious than a man. Any woman. I can say that too."[13]

X.G.   *Can we say that only women write completely?*

M.D.   Yes. Maybe it's only women who write.

X.G.   *Anyway, I think that men writers, to write, have to be women, don't they?*

M.D.   Oh, yes, that's certain, or else it becomes a Montherlantian horror.[14]

X.G.   *That's what it is, yes.*

M.D.   It's over. It's really pretty good. It's over.

X.G.   *But then, this movement that carries you toward the light—I don't know how you said it; those sentences were so beautiful—but anyway, what you said in them . . .*

M.D. I tried to be clear.

X.G. *Is it . . .*

M.D. But I realize—I had reread all of that before seeing you—I realize that when I speak about myself, I'm speaking about a woman. [*End of tape.*]

Second Interview

X.G. *It's hard for me to talk about* La Femme du Gange, *having just read the script. It's put me in utter shock. I feel that it's the ultimate of what you could write. It's never been so strong, so beautiful, so disturbing; that is, that one loses oneself so much inside it. I'm totally lost. I have to tell you: there's a word that bothered me.*

M.D. "Impossible?"

X.G. *No, "Heroes"; at one point you say, "The heroes of the ball." Because everything that happens and everything you say has nothing at all to do with heroes; the person no longer exists; identifying with a person isn't possible.*

M.D. I looked. I remember looking for the word, and I didn't find it.

X.G. *You see why I'm telling you this—it's just a word, it's a detail— because on the whole, I felt lost: as a* person, *such a thing didn't exist anymore, and that's why the word "hero" is almost shocking. Since it's the opposite of that.*[15] *In the script of* La Femme du Gange, *individuals don't exist anymore, since desire passes from one to another and it doesn't belong to one any more than to another.*

M.D. Yes, and also, in heroism, there's a will to be heroic, whereas here there is none. Everybody is subjected [to what happens]. People told me that the film was a suicide. Some young people saw it at Digne; they got together and then came to see me. They were extremely hostile, as if I hadn't deserved my film. It's strange. They told me to

33

bottle it up, not to show it to anyone, because no one, except them at eighteen, could understand it. That really frightened me because they said, "After this, there's nothing left for you to do." So I said, "I'm going to try to do something else." I was trying to save my skin. And they said, "Okay, try."

X.G.   *That's because one gets to this ultimate point that's nearly unbearable, and you almost have the impression that you can't go any further. Things have never been as bare before.*

M.D.   There are four books together.

X.G.   *There's* L'Amour, Le Vice-consul, Le Ravissement.

M.D.   And the film. There are three books and a film.

X.G.   *I know that for me it's these three books—along with* Détruire, *but definitely these three books—that overwhelmed me the most, that touched me the most. They aren't put together, but what's most intense is picked up from each one.*

M.D.   As if they're sort of scorched. Because each of their stories is discounted, except the story of the ball.

X.G.   *The story of the ball, which is always the beginning.*

M.D.   And then there's the couple that I've always neglected: Michael Richardson and Anne-Marie Stretter.

X.G.   *. . . and who appear there, on the scene.*

M.D.   It's a question of a few lines, in *Le Ravissement* and in *Le Vice-consul,* a few lines.

X.G.   *In* Le Vice-consul, *this woman really fascinated me. She's very impressive. But why, do you think, did they talk about suicide? Whose?*

M.D.   They said that what they were looking for was to be themselves, and that *I* had succeeded in being me, and that to succeed in that is a suicide; it was a suicide of all the other possible selves.

X.G.   *So maybe that's what I meant when I said there was no identity anymore.*

M.D.   Yes, maybe it's by virtue of not existing. I believe that sometimes.

X.G.   *No, on the contrary, it is an existence, it's the strongest existence.*

Identity, I mean, someone who would believe himself to be in control of himself, of his desires, being a whole and secure person, having a will and all that—that's lost.

M.D. Are you talking about them or me? Because when I say that I don't exist, it's because I myself don't exist that that can exist so much . . .

X.G. . . . *can pass.*

M.D. . . . those people.

X.G. *They don't give the illusion that you get from most novels, and films too, that they're whole people.*

M.D. They're completely mismatched, dislodged from society, completely.

X.G. *And that's why it's so frightening; it's that they're so totally pervaded by something that's stronger than they are, which is desire.*

M.D. That's what it is, it's a kind of detachment, but organic in any case, physical. Something happened to them that got them out of there. But what?

X.G. *Certainly for the reader—at least, for me—that's it too, that it forces me not to be so fond of myself. That's why it frightens me at the same time. The way they are pervaded by that, the book pervades me.*

M.D. So you recognize something then?

X.G. *Of myself?*

M.D. Vaguely? Something you would have wanted?

X.G. *But I recognize everything. Entirely . . . not something that's identical to me, but something that is what's inside me and that maybe I try to mask, by living, to seal off.*

M.D. Because usually a refusal of society is something revolutionary; it's political. Here too, probably.

X.G. *Completely political.*

M.D. Completely political, but not devised. A refusal of society is violent; it expresses itself through a departure, a refusal, a given action. But it's not the same here. They're immersed in the refusal, and I don't

35

see how it began, how they became separated from society. It's like a birth, always; furthermore, there are parturitions. It's like a liquid world.

x.g. *But how is there this kind of accident every time?*

m.d. . . . which precedes refusal and separation? I don't know—that's what's strange. I find them already in place. When I began the film of *L'Amour,* it was already there. So you have to suppose that there had been a book before this, one that I hadn't noticed or that didn't interest me. A book that would be this separation, the separation from society, which would have to do with the fact of separation. But in the books that I've written, they're already separated and have been for a very, very long time.

x.g. *But aren't the books that you wrote before what allows this to be written? I'm thinking of* Les Petits Chevaux, *for example, which I've just read. In the end, I'm really glad to have read your other books before because I sense that something is going to take shape here and that somehow everything is in place. For example, what crushes them in* Les Petits Chevaux *is the sun.*

m.d. Yes, they're separated, already, by the sun.

x.g. *That allows them, afterward, to live that, to enter the space where they live—for instance, the people in* La Femme du Gange.

m.d. That's quite possible. I never thought of that.

x.g. *And at the same time, in* Les Petits Chevaux, *it's still a book that's less frightening. It's closer to the books that can be written.*

m.d. Yes, there's nothing frightening about it at all.

x.g. *But one knows, once having read your other books, that that can happen, that everything can happen from that point on, because* Les Petits Chevaux *is still preoccupied with things around it.*

m.d. Oh, and it's also psychological.

x.g. *Yes, and then later on all that settles, the useless things and all the psychologizing. That's why one is confronted so brutally, so directly by what happens in* L'Amour *and* Le Ravissement.

m.d. I find that *Le Marin de Gilbraltar* sets this up more than *Les Petits Chevaux.*

36

X.G. *Yes,* Le Marin de Gibraltar *as well. I've thought particularly that the woman's love for the sailor, the completely nonexistent being who nevertheless exists with an enormous amount of force . . .*

M.D. This state of being reprieved . . . you see, whatever love she lives is contained in her waiting for a love, for the love of the sailor of Gibraltar. That's already related to what I'm doing now. But obviously there's a world of difference between *Les Petits Chevaux de Tarquinia* and *Le Femme du Gange.*

X.G. *What would be interesting to know is the itinerary you followed that allowed you, basically, to tear yourself away from all that.*

M.D. I thought that's what had to be done.

X.G. *And it was certainly more reassuring.*

M.D. Oh, I could write a book like that in two weeks. I could be that crass, I really could. It's a kind of facility; I used to have it in school, you know, the same thing. I can whip off a book in three weeks, any kind of book. *La Musica,* which was performed all over the world, is in that vein.

X.G. *Yes, it's the same; one also feels what might be coming, but we're not there yet.*

M.D. *Suzanna Andler* already stands out a lot more against the background of death. But it's also still very facile. It's strange about that; there are those two things. For a very long time, I was very sociable. I would have dinner at people's houses. It was a whole thing: I used to go to cocktail parties, I'd see people there . . . and I wrote those books. It was like that. And then, one time, I had a love affair, and I think that's when everything changed. I don't believe I've told you about it, have I?

X.G. *No.*

M.D. It was an erotic experience that was very, very, very violent—how do you describe it?—I went through a crisis that was . . . suicidal; that is . . . what I tell in *Moderato cantabile,* this woman who wants to be killed, I lived that . . . and from that point on, my books changed. I've been thinking about this for two or three years; I think that the turn, the veering toward . . . toward sincerity happened then. And, as in *Moderato cantabile*, the personality of the man I was living with didn't count. Really, it wasn't a story . . . I mean a love story, but it was—what is the word?—a sexual story. I thought I would never get out of it. It was very strange. Because in *Moderato cantabile* I told it from the outside, but I've never spoken about it any other way. Oh, I did talk about it to one or two people, but only vaguely; I never really went into it. Well, so what happened? Why? Why did that take away the facility?

X.G.   *It was a rupture with a whole entourage, with a kind of tranquillity.*

M.D.   It was a radical rupture. I continued to lead a social life and then one day . . . or rather, little by little, that completely stopped.

X.G.   *Did you have the impression at that time, in the affair, of being submerged in something stronger?*

M.D.   Oh yes, it was stronger than I was.

X.G.   *And was that the first time you'd had that feeling?*

M.D.   Yes—that is, I had been through dangerous periods in my life, I know, but I'd never lived them consciously, whereas at that point, I knew clearly what I wanted. This theme comes back constantly.

X.G.   *Yes, that's what it is.*

M.D.   In *Hiroshima* there was already "You kill me." I had written it, but I had never, ever lived it.

X.G.   *And yet how one* feels *it in* Hiroshima!

M.D.   And it was the year after that that I wrote *Moderato cantabile*. I would like to make that a film. Say, that's an idea.

X.G.   *Without writing it first?*

M.D.   No. Make *Moderato cantabile* a film. To remake it, on a low budget. Anyway, that's another issue.

X.G.   *But since* Moderato cantabile, *hasn't your writing, your way of saying things, settled?*

M.D.   Yes, very much so.

X.G.   *It's gone more and more toward a stripping away of all that's really extraneous.*

M.D.   Yes, but you see, that's how it's been in my life, too. I think that the life I lead is sometimes, is so . . . hard . . . I think . . . looking from the outside, it's hard to be with writing, the way I am . . . or with film . . . yes, I'll finish my sentence: . . . so hard that I wear myself out. I probably should slow down a little. It's hard especially because—not especially; it's hard *also*—because people don't understand what I do. There's a general silence surrounding me. That adds to the solitude, necessarily. Anyway, this doesn't matter so much, really. Living is hard . . . very hard.

X.G. *But don't you think that if people misunderstand or refuse to understand and bury you in silence it's because they don't want to be confronted with that so brutally, that such a confrontation is very, very difficult to accept?*

M.D. Maybe. Oh, there are still a lot of readers, I have to say, who understand, who get inside, I mean . . . maybe understand isn't the word. But I'm known in relation to what I do. That's really strange, too. I'm well known but not from the inside. I'm known around my work, you see, and often for the wrong reasons.

X.G. *Yes, that's quite possible. I've had the impression several times that when people say your name, everyone immediately says, "Yes, yes, Marguerite Duras," but when it comes to saying what's in your books, there's no one there. It's as if people just know about you. They know you exist somewhere, and then when it comes to getting into your texts . . . there could be a fear there.*

M.D. All that will happen very naturally, I think, after I'm dead. But I attract misogynist reactions in a very particular way.

X.G. *That doesn't surprise me. Precisely because I think your books are utterly revolutionary, totally avant-garde, both from the usual revolutionary point of view and from a woman's point of view, and most people haven't gotten that far yet.*

M.D. Yes, it's twice as intolerable.

X.G. *Yes. And maybe it's the only true calling into question, since we've already seen a lot of things on a revolutionary level, a lot of things said or movements or things done, but not by a woman. Which is not to say that at the same time there isn't . . . The social calling*

39

into question in general is uniquely social; it's not also about the female sex or person.

M.D. But to call society into question is still to accept it. It's like movies about war: in all war movies, there's a secret adoration of war.

X.G. *Yes, so then it's not "called into question."*

M.D. I mean that people who are involved in this, who write about a refusal of society, carry a kind of nostalgia within themselves. I'm sure they're much less separated from it than I am. I'm absolutely sure.

X.G. *Yes, yes. And then they write the same way; they write against a society . . .*

M.D. That's right, as if from inside, from within a society.

X.G. *They use the same language and that doesn't make society explode; it doesn't make it disappear. But with you, it does.*

M.D. Wherever I go, I see signs of society's death everywhere. It's like hallucinating.

X.G. *Yes, and you reveal them. Again, that's why it's so completely frightening.*

M.D. In everyday life, when I watch the news on television, it's already like an "after"; it's as if they were speaking . . . You know, there's a story that goes like this: there's a man who forgets that the stairs end, so he keeps climbing beyond the stairway. Well, so all these officials, all these terrible men who are so terrible to see and hear, they're all dead and don't know it.

X.G. *They didn't realize it.*

M.D. And when you begin to see things from this angle, it's terrifying. All these people who want to earn money, it's like they're trying to get even with it, to get even with death, but I know that it's too late, it's over. Sometimes you think you're dreaming when you hear them. In bistros, or fancy restaurants on the few occasions you go there, when you hear the bourgeoisie speak, it too is speaking above the stairway, in a zone that's detached from reality.

X.G. *And they don't realize that what's underneath has been worn away.*

M.D. Yes, that's it exactly.

X.G. *And that's what your books do too; they do the work of mining; they mine from below.*

M.D. But I see reality as mined. And in film, too, there's a kind of return to the elements of nature, the sand, and the sea; there aren't ever streets, you've noticed. It's people . . . there are houses, but they're empty, as they would be afterward; there are hotels, but they're closed down.

X.G. *And even the sand, like what would remain after . . .*

M.D. That's what's going to remain. Maybe at the bottom of all this there's also—because a single reason never accounts for everything, isn't valid, doesn't explain everything by itself—an immense political despair.

X.G. *. . . you mean the feeling that it's not worth the trouble to get involved in . . . in everything that's so-called revolutionary, everything that's supposedly opposed to society?*

M.D. Yes, because it's an old mechanism.

X.G. *So true.*

M.D. It's forever beginning again . . . all the time, to the letter. It's unreal, the extent to which all political discourses resemble one another.

X.G. *Yes, that's what it is; it's the same discourse, conveyed by everyone from time to time; it's the wrong and the right side, but it's the same thing.*

M.D. It's the same thing.

X.G. *It's the same outline, the same way of speaking.*

M.D. Nobody offers anything new, some new way, not even a tiny one.

X.G. *Yes, you do, in what you write. Because I believe that it's a beginning to renounce this illusion of speech, of decision and of struggle in confrontation with something that resembles you—all right, to renounce all that, and to begin by listening to what's working on us from the inside. And if we don't start with that, we don't do anything but repeat what's going on on the outside and what's always been going on.*

M.D. But would it be something from the unconscious or from beyond?

X.G. *Yes, from the unconscious. I see it as listening to the unconscious.*

> *The unconscious is desire, and that's what speaks within us, in our place. And in your books, that's the voice that speaks; it speaks in the characters but for them, and that's the only truth that exists, finally. Everything we try to say consciously, with a protest or something like that, muffles this voice so that it can't come through.*

M.D.   It's in order to fill up the holes, yes, the ruins.

X.G.   *Yes, exactly, but they come through in your texts; they appear in your films.*

M.D.   It's a world in ruins, in my films.

X.G.   *Yes, everything has caved in.*

M.D.   But they don't have any personal desires, no *desiderata*. A story comes along, a traveler arrives, he throws himself onto the story, he weds himself to it, and afterward . . . they become vacant again. For the duration of the film, they could graft themselves that way indefinitely onto any story at all. Maybe that's what life is: to enter within, to let oneself be carried along by this story—this story, well, the story of others—in a constant movement of . . . how do you describe it, when you're carried off from a place?

X.G.   *. . . abduction, ravishing.*

M.D.   Yes, that's what it is.

X.G.   *It's this word "ravishing" that you used; one is "ravished" from oneself; one is "ravished" from others.*[16]

M.D.   That's what's best. That's what's most desirable in the world.

X.G.   *Of course.*

M.D.   That's what never happens in life.

X.G.   *Or very, very rarely.*

M.D.   Yes, at extreme moments.

X.G.   *Yes, of rupture, of vacancy, of receptivity. But I think that all that is political; I mean that if you don't begin with this, then it's not worth . . . continuing, because otherwise, you* only *continue. If you don't begin by being invaded with this emptiness, this gaping.*

M.D.   Do you think it exists in everyone?

X.G.   *Oh yes, it exists in everyone. It's cleverly or not cleverly hidden, depending on the person.*

42

M.D. Is it desire?

X.G. *Yes, it's desire as a force that doesn't belong to us.*

M.D. Or *jouissance*—what is called *jouissance*, the search for *jouissance*.

X.G. *I think they're two different things.*

M.D. It's still about the mother, isn't it?

X.G. *Yes . . . but at that point, the mother is something we know we've lost, and of which we know that everything that happens to us will only be a . . .*

M.D. Yes, whereas here, it's not about a lost paradise.

X.G. *Right, it's different.*

M.D. It's not about any kind of paradise. It's about a situation of man in relation to himself, a reflexive situation.

X.G. *And in fact, maybe in* Le Marin de Gibraltar, *you could still think there was a paradise: that is, the moment when the woman would have known the sailor, but we don't know after all whether it's mythical or real.*

M.D. Yes, she created him out of whole cloth.

X.G. *So that could be an illusion of paradise: this man exists somewhere; you know you won't find him. When she rejects men, after making love with them, she says: "That's not the one."*[17] *She knows she won't find him, but she still thinks he might exist.*

M.D. She put him there for herself, in life, like a sort of unattainable man, a man-God.

X.G. *That would still be a possible paradise.*

M.D. Yes, whereas afterward, it's all over. But speaking of that, I remember people being furious with me when I'd given Gallimard the book *Le Marin.* Queneau really bawled me out fiercely—I even cried—because he said that it was Romanticism.[18]

X.G. *If you just recount the plot, if you say for example that there's a woman who sees, let's say, an ideal man as if she had known him and looks for him everywhere, you can call that romantic. But in fact, if you read the book, it's really about something else. And the proof is what happened afterward; the proof is the books you've written.*

43

M.D. I find that *Le Marin de Gibraltar* in its treatment of things is strongly anchored in the real.

X.G. *Yes, but your books become more and more materialist, materialist books in the Marxist sense, no longer idealist at all.*

M.D. Like *Le Square* as well; it has the same materialist vein. *Le Square* is about the theory of needs. People generally take it for a love story.

X.G. *As a matter of fact, I was thinking, something that bothered me is that you can have a book called* L'Amour, *because it's in* L'Amour *that you say, "There's no word for that." Well, it almost seemed wounding to me that you could say "l'amour," especially in a title.*

M.D. And you were upset before or after reading it?

X.G. *After. I didn't pay that much attention in the beginning. I simply read the book. And afterward I realized that—for me—what mattered was so much the suspension of this love, the unsaid of this love, everything that circulates through this love, that it was almost brutal to name it. Is it brutal to say this to you?*

M.D. No, no. You're right. The title is out of reaction. It came afterward, when the book was finished. The title is a reaction against similar titles.

X.G. *Oh, I see—for once, after the word "love," one can enter into something else? Is that it?*

M.D. Yes. In any case, into whatever you want, only not a love story, not an unfolding.

X.G. *Of course, exactly.*

M.D. *La Femme du Gange* . . . yes . . . that's a fair distance from *L'Amour*, a fair distance.

X.G. *There's a lot of the book in it, even so.*

M.D. The woman in it, in black, dressed in black—she doesn't exist in *L'Amour*, it seems to me; I don't know anymore.

X.G. *In* L'Amour *there's only one woman; that's different already.*

M.D. She's the one who's sick.

X.G. *She's the one who's sick.*

M.D. She's the remains, she's what's left over from someone.

X.G. *Yes, and at the same time . . .*

M.D. All of them, you could say, are remains—what other people would call remains. What, from the outside, one might call remains I would call the main thing.

X.G. *Exactly. When everything has been evacuated from what masks . . . But the woman in* L'Amour, *she's carrying a child, there are the child's cries. I noticed that, that in* L'Amour *there's a woman carrying a child and that in* Le Vice-consul *there's also a woman carrying a child, the woman who walks and who—I remember, it's just amazing—who's looking for directions in order to get lost; it's crazy. But I don't know why these two babies in the bellies of two women disappeared from* La Femme du Gange. *I just happened to notice that.*

M.D. The child cried from the inside, you see; he also inhabited the place, from the inside. I think he got replaced by the voices.

X.G. *You mean, it was still a question of something that was too heavy, too full?*

M.D. There was something in that woman that continually waited for children, for children whom she would leave behind the sea wall, I remember—isn't that it?—and then society came and took them; it was a very clear image and they populated the land. You could say she was too functional for *La Femme du Gange.* I was supposed to find Lol. V. Stein, as she was at the S. Thala ball, naked. Children would have interfered with that.

X.G. *Yes, they'd be too cumbersome.*

M.D. So, she's not the woman in *L'Amour,* not entirely. Are you sorry about that?

X.G. *No. No, no.*

M.D. I think she was replaced: she gave birth to the voices. I think that one of the voices is she.

X.G. *But, in fact, this woman in black who speaks . . . you say, "who speaks for the others and who speaks quite loudly, as if we weren't going to hear her . . ."*

M.D. Yes, as in *Détruire,* already, in the film. They speak loudly. The confidential tone is cut out, completely. Only the social tone is

45

there.[19] It's as if they didn't know how to speak. In *La Femme du Gange*, it's as if she had completely forgotten how to speak to people. She speaks softly, she doesn't look at them like people: she comes, she comes to within a foot of him and looks at him the way you'd look at a tree, at any kind of material object. She doesn't know how to live anymore. There were some people who were shocked by the woman's public voice. It was totally intentional on my part, totally. She says everything in the same tone, she speaks as if by rote. But when I talk about the voice, I mean the scorched voice, the *voice-off* . . . they're not from the women.

X.G. *Ah yes, I'd like to hear them. But the way you present them—if you can say that, because how do you present something that's burnt to ashes?—the way you speak about them in the beginning, it's crazy . . . And at the same time, they are two voices and they're twins, you say: they're very close to one another.*

M.D. They're very close, yes.

X.G. *But they would still have to be split; it can't be the same voice.*

M.D. No, it can't because there's still a . . . a relation between them. They are two girls who live in the garret of a hotel, as I see it; they're eighteen years old, like Alissa, and have been for a long time, a very long time. It's the opposite of the woman in black—they're in white, you see, as I see them. It's like another movie, not yet filmed. And I can see very clearly into the hotel where they are, when I'm back there; they are totally concrete . . . in rags . . . forgotten.

X.G. *They're the ones who can tell. Because they're forgotten, they can speak.*

M.D. For me, the film is more than anything just that: these two voices. I find that they're what's most important in the book, what they say.

X.G. *Didn't they take on a little bit of the role that Stein had in* Détruire?

M.D. No, because they never act on the situation.

X.G. *They're set back even further from it?*

M.D. Completely set back.

X.G. *But because he, in some way, was also speaking, could also say*

46

something. But finally, maybe he existed a bit too much.

M.D. He was there, you could see him; he had connections with
Alissa . . . certain connections, whereas the girls are really on the
top floor of the film.

X.G. *And, as you see it, why two women, two young women?*

M.D. That's a mystery—I don't know. Because . . . they don't have
offspring, it stops with them . . . I think. They're sterile. I think
that's what it is. The end.

X.G. *It wouldn't be the same with boys?*

M.D. Two boys?

X.G. *Yes. Instead of the two girls.*

M.D. No, it wouldn't be the same. They would never see what the girls
see; the odors of algae and of rain, boys wouldn't smell them. Those
rains over the sea that the girls invent, "It's raining on the sea"—it's
not raining, the boys wouldn't see. The boys, no, they wouldn't be in
the same boat, they wouldn't be in the same boat, merged with the
sea, merged . . . They would play a role, you see. They wouldn't be
in that passive state.
[*The tape stops. We don't notice for a long time. A lot of things are
lost. We try to pick up again.*]

M.D. You were saying, "Silence, I think, is disparaged, maybe." I said,
"Passivity is a disparaged, discredited word."

X.G. *Discredited.*

M.D. And you say that passivity is silence.

X.G. *It amounts to the same thing, that is that men do things in such a
way that you can't hear, since they're speaking.*

M.D. That's a considerable strength. Imagine what the world would be if
we opposed passivity to . . . to all the stupidity, to all the rulers,
to . . . to all men as well. Yes, I was talking about passive voices; I
don't remember what I was saying. The voices in *La Femme du
Gange* are passive; they never intervene. No one intervenes, for that
matter, in *La Femme du Gange.* The voices come from another time.
I say that, I think, in the preface.

47

[*Voice off:* "Where's my mother?" *M.D.:* "She's here."]

X.G. *Yes, you spoke about the park, actually, as an example of this passivity.*

M.D. If there had been a man in Isabelle Granger's house, the film simply wouldn't have existed.[20] The man would have prevented it . . . prevented the film from being. I'll give an example: Isabelle Granger is in the park while the traveling salesman is crying; she's in the park, she clings to the park. You think: she's in the park. There's a profound interrelation between the park and the woman, her movements. If there were a man in the park like that, you'd think: the man has gone to think things over in the park. He's gone to resolve his problems and to be alone in order to think, to philoso-phize, or whatever you like. So, you see, the opening gets closed off; it's already much narrower, whereas the woman is simply in the park. This kind of state, which leaves everything open all around— all around the fact, so to speak, or whatever—would have disap-peared. If the house in *Nathalie Granger* wasn't a house of women and only that, a house of women . . . if a man, of whatever kind, had been living there, in the house, the film wouldn't have been possible. It would have been as if there were a witness. Because I have this feeling about *Nathalie Granger* that men shouldn't see what happens there. A very strong feeling.

X.G. *Because in the end they can't understand a world of women?*

M.D. Yes, it's airtight; we trail along together, but there are walls between them and us.

X.G. *Yes, that's also what you were saying about this complicity, this understanding between the two women, being in something like a liquid.*

M.D. Yes. You were asking me if what was between them was a relation of . . . of love, that is, of desire.

X.G. *Yes, between the two women.*

M.D. I don't think so. There're two movements of women in a single place and . . . yes, I think a lot of men, when the film is shown, will see this as a "release" of women in a zoo . . . but so far the film has

48

generally had a violent effect on men. As if they had perceived in it things they hadn't seen before, like what happens once they've left—that is, when the door is closed. Yes, I was telling you that what I . . . yes, that the women were enclosed in a container which would be the house, in the same liquid. I find that the light that's in the water, the house diked up that way by the walls . . . Obviously, in the end, it opens up as if around an axis, the kitchen door and the front door, and everything spills out. Yes, I was telling you that what I had against the film was that it was a bit like a lesson for people who film women, who film them as coquettish, as . . . as made-up, as feminine women.

x.g. *Yes, and not as women who iron and who . . .*

m.d. That's right, women in a functional femininity, in femininity . . . in the service of man. You see women loved by men, seen by men, and so on, coveted or rejected, and that's it, whereas I have them ironing, washing dishes . . . it's a little like a film that's inside out, meaning that I show everything that normally isn't shown. Like the negative of the usual film where women come into play. It's something I reproach myself for a little, since it's somewhat didactic this way.

x.g. *Yes, but it was also important for that to be there, because if it's not usually shown, that's a kind of esthetic prejudice.*

m.d. But then no, since women's work is degraded.

x.g. *Of course, because it's not pretty; it's not at all interesting.*

m.d. That's right. The man is shown at work, at his office, phoning someone, and meanwhile the woman's in her boudoir. And also the way leisure comes into the picture, I showed that or tried to show it; can you tell that in the film? I'm not aware of the violence of the image. It's all from the woman's perspective, from woman's secret life . . . from her secret and public life.

x.g. *But for me, I don't know, I think that it was the first time I'd ever seen it shown anywhere. Certainly I may have felt it in my life, but . . . it's true that I had never felt it that way in a film, in a text, anywhere.*

49

M.D. There are two movements, and sometimes they come together. The two movements come together and then separate; it's like one and the same person, you see.

X.G. *Yes, a splitting-in-two.*

M.D. I'm thinking of when Isabelle Granger is listening to the voice on the radio and when the other . . . when her friend comes behind the window with her arms full of kindling; also when they speak to each other from one room to another. These movements . . . it's very simple—it's also quite complicated though . . . In a sense, apparently, that's how it's treated; it's treated . . . as if I had been filming cats in the garden, you see.

X.G. *But that, I think, is like women's lives, which apparently are very simple—taking care of the house—but which are really complicated.*

M.D. And then again what's brewing under this . . . silence, this passivity, this . . . this ordinary everyday work. What's also brewing . . . well, the violence at the end of the film, when she tears up everything with the greatest calm. I don't know whether I said this before but . . .

X.G. *I don't think so. I don't think so; it's precisely this calm violence that you said a man wouldn't have.*

M.D. No. It's unthinkable.

X.G. *People would treat him as if he were crazy.*

M.D. Right, a man would never have listened to the traveling salesman the way the women do, unless he were crazy, stuck at home because of mental illness.

X.G. *No, he wouldn't have listened; he would have thrown him out, yelling, which is to say that he would have used the salesman's own weapons . . . The salesman comes to speak, to say something, and a man would have said something too, just as stereotypical, but not the women.*

M.D. And then again, you still have to come back to an elementary grammar of the image, or of . . . of . . . how do you name this realm? I don't know . . . a woman inhabits a place completely; a woman's presence fills a place. A man travels through it; he doesn't really inhabit it. I don't know what level we're on here. Meta-physical,[21] do you suppose?

x.g.   *Oh, not at all. I think we're on a very physical level, a very real level.*

m.d.   No, because it's completely . . . at the level of the direct image where this happens . . . the direct image that I'm talking about, about the consequence of the image. When Isabelle Granger is in that room with the children's things in her hand, in her hands, the room is filled with her, up to the ceiling . . . by her alone.

x.g.   *Yes, you might even say she creates the room.*

m.d.   That's it, exactly. And it's an incredible joy to show that. I was very sensitive to this, to this work, of showing it in *Nathalie Granger*. And then, what people always tell me as they leave the film is, "Oh that could have gone on for another two hours," and they think they're talking about the movie, but in fact they're talking about the women.

x.g.   *Yes, and it could go on for a lifetime even!*

m.d.   Exactly. It's funny because it's . . . what I'm showing there is very daily, very everyday, it's . . . this happens hundreds and millions of times everyday but people don't show it. It's true that they've just discovered the behavior of cats; we didn't know about them before. And that's the animal most familiar to us . . .

x.g.   *People are going to discover women's behavior! But it's true that we haven't begun to discover the way women live.*

m.d.   I was thinking, you see, that progress has been made, even so. The women do dishes for four minutes, and there's *one* sentence spoken: they say, "We have to remember to call the mayor's office." It's a nothing sentence, it doesn't make any sense. Listen, five years ago, I could never have gotten away with that; people would have said, "It's monotonous, why show women doing dishes?"

x.g.   *You would have filled up the silence?*

m.d.   No, I'd have been telling the viewer quite frankly to go screw himself. Now, everyone understands that I did it. There's not a young person, not a single viewer, old or young, who's said to me

51

yet, "The dishwashing is too long." They all understand the meaning I gave it. Nearly six minutes pass between clearing off the table and doing the dishes. So there's been enormous progress; it's very encouraging.

X.G.   *Yes, it's true.*

M.D.   It has to be done. Because still I use big stars, Lucia Bose and Jeanne Moreau. And instead of having them "act," I show them from the back. I show their hands for ten minutes.

X.G.   *How do they react, by the way? I'm curious about that. I was thinking, you know, Jeanne Moreau . . .*

M.D.   They were delighted, and happy to film that.

X.G.   *They understood?*

M.D.   Completely.

X.G.   *Because it's true that women like that who are so used to having extravagant roles, all show . . .*

M.D.   Right. With Jeanne, her roles are usually like a festival. She adored this deaf role, you see, deaf and dumb.

X.G.   *That's really interesting because a star is precisely the kind of woman at the other end of this . . .*

M.D.   At the other end.

X.G.   *. . . who only shows what's staring you in the face.*

M.D.   And at the end of the film, she says to me, "Margot, when are we going to begin again?" And she told me that during the filming, she never even once had the spells of nausea that she usually has. And I think, myself, that the house in *Nathalie Granger* is a cavern, a cave.

X.G.   *Oh, yes, that's like what I was saying a while ago. It's like a uterus with twin girls inside who float a little in that liquid. I don't know what that fluid is called; do you know?*

M.D.   The waters.

X.G.   *The waters, that's right, because afterward they say that her water broke. That would be the end, when the doors open. And you were also saying after that, when you were moving toward* La Femme du Gange, *it bursts open . . .*

52

M.D. It explodes. That is, if you asked me where Nathalie Granger's house is, I'd say that it's among the empty villas you see in *La Femme du Gange*. I couldn't stand keeping on with that film. I finished *Nathalie Granger* in July; I wrote *La Femme du Gange* in September, and I shot it in November. I couldn't stay on the terrain of *Nathalie Granger* at all, which I still see as a didactic terrain. Really, it's a complex film, but—it's been said, at least; I don't have to say it—it isn't completely, completely mine. It's as if I were telling people, "You'll see what I can do when I talk about women and also maybe what should be done." That's what it's like. But I really wasn't in my element. Whereas in *La Femme du Gange*, it was like being at home. *Nathalie Granger* is a little like a revised and corrected version of other people's films.

X.G. *Yes, perhaps you* say *more in* Nathalie Granger—*but saying is still . . . I don't know . . . saying, teaching—and it's true that it's much less you.*[22]

M.D. They're words addressed to others, even so.

X.G. *Yes, whereas in* La Femme du Gange, *all that is broken up, burst open.*

M.D. Yes, it's a boat . . . that has departed. It's the opposite of the house; they never return anywhere.

X.G. *Yes, they're in an uninhabitable place, where you can't live.*

M.D. Yes, where you can't live.

X.G. *On that level, it's the opposite.*

M.D. Exactly. People asked me, in fact (this is off the track), people talked to my assistant a lot, and he's asked me to publish them together because he finds it interesting that one follows on the other. [*Silence.*] Well, anyway I have to go do the shopping. [*Silence.*] Has a lot been lost?

Third Interview

X.G.   *We could begin, so that we don't forget about it—although it's not very pleasant to talk about, and that's precisely why we might tend to forget it—with what happened when you did* Hiroshima, mon amour.

M.D.   It was the first time I worked in film, and I didn't know that the percentage clause existed, of course, since I'd never signed a film contract. I didn't have any money, and I did all the work, the screenplay and dialogue, for a million francs, a million *old* francs.[23] And ten years later, Resnais told me that in ten years I must have lost millions—twenty-two million, I think. At the time, I had absolutely no money. We had so little money we couldn't even go on vacation. I believe now that if I hadn't been a woman, they wouldn't have . . . robbed me—and that's the only word for it—the way they did.

X.G.   *It's despicable. Because they're under the impression, I suppose, that women don't know anything about it, don't know anything about business, about money, and so they can justify doing it.*

M.D.   Because it's a total mystery nonetheless; why no one—including Resnais, I have to say—why no one told me, "Don't forget to ask for a 'percentage.' "[24]

X.G.   *That's just crazy!*

M.D.   Why didn't anyone tell me?

X.G.   *. . . when you were the crucial person. It's obvious that the film*

55

couldn't have been made if there hadn't been the basis of the story, the text.

M.D.   It wouldn't have been the same film. But I could have written the story the same way for other directors. I don't see why authors in the film-production line are so . . . count for so little, when people say that they're 50 percent of everything.

X.G.   *I don't know, maybe it's just a contempt for—well, in the best sense of the term—for culture.*

M.D.   It's maybe . . . the story, they don't realize the importance of the story, perhaps. The film is a processing of the story. The film was Resnais's work, which he could have done exactly the same way no matter what the story; I think that's what it is.

X.G.   *And still, even the word "story"—I don't know if that works for* Hiroshima . . .

M.D.   We could say scenario.

X.G.   *. . . because it is a story, but not in the traditional sense of something that's told.*

M.D.   It's like a preamble . . . that is, no, the story took place.

X.G.   *It's not told in a traditionally chronological and linear way, about things happening one after another, and there's a kind of doubling of the story that takes place.*

M.D.   In Hiroshima. The story of Hiroshima doubles the story of Nevers. Yes, that's it. I've just been to see it again, and that's what I'm still most pleased about, when the Japanese man, while speaking of the German, says to her, "When I am dead, where are you?" and she says, "In the cave," something like that. The Japanese man says instead and in place of the German, "When I am dead, do you scream?"—that's it, "When I'm dead, do you scream?"—and she says, "You are dead," yes.[25]

X.G.   *Yes, that is, already at that time, desire was circulating from person to person, not indiscriminately, but still it could pass from one person to another.*

M.D.   Yes, I was struck by that and also by the refusal that Riva represents, the woman of Nevers.

56

X.G.   *Yes, up against the whole society.*

M.D.   Up against the whole society, she had always refused what they had
       done to her, and she rediscovers the anger she felt in Nevers—
       uncut like a diamond—and her pain, but her anger as well; the
       anger remained, it's flawless. That really struck me when I saw it
       again, and it hasn't aged in that respect.

X.G.   *No, absolutely not. I also saw it again a little while ago. It was
       showing in Paris, and I said to myself—I had been so impressed
       when I'd seen it the first time, to the point of having a hysterical
       reaction, that is, feeling my body injured, feeling . . . completely . . .
       sick in a physical way—and I wondered what effect it would have
       on me. It had the same effect on me, just as strong. And strangely, I
       had the feeling that I didn't remember very much—well, I remem-
       bered the story and all that—and when I heard it, well, when I saw
       it, I could have recited everything she said along with her. I
       remembered all the words, but only at that moment; it's crazy!*

M.D.   And how long was it afterward?

X.G.   *I had seen it when it came out. What was the date? I never know
       dates.*

M.D.   Oh yes, then it was thirteen years ago, fourteen years. It was the
       same year I wrote *Moderato cantabile*. I wrote the two things in the
       same year. Since *Moderato cantabile* was filmed immediately after-
       ward, I remember.

X.G.   *Ah, I thought so too. And then that it's Jeanne Moreau who acts in*
       Moderato cantabile *and you put Jeanne Moreau in* Nathalie Granger
       in a role that's completely the opposite—well, not the opposite of
       Moderato cantabile *but the opposite of the roles she usually plays,
       that is, of movie-star roles.*

M.D.   Yes, there's not a single purple passage; there's nothing, nothing; it's
       a completely mute role. And it's strange, the first thing she said to
       me after the film, when we were saying goodbye, she said, "Margot,
       when do we begin again?"26 She usually has moments of depression
       during her films, she's very intelligent, I think she perceives the
       rottenness under the [*unintelligible word*] that they do to her in

57

commercial films, but with this film she was always even-tempered, very at ease, very happy.

x.g.　*I don't know how you direct a film because I've never seen you, but wouldn't she usually feel that she's being treated as an object?*

m.d.　Yes, she's often said that on television, too, that the way film directors treat actresses is unbelievable, horrible.

x.g.　*Did she feel better doing* Nathalie Granger?

m.d.　Yes, she was better. She was really, really fine there. We've known each other for a long time, too, I should add. And then, when she had read the script, she was the one who telephoned me, saying, "If Lucia Bose doesn't do it, I want to." And finally, when my assistant came to see me, that's what I told him; I said to him, "Listen I'd really like to have both of them." He shouted with joy and I got them both. And I have to say that Lucia and Jeanne got along together perfectly.

x.g.　*So the complicity we see between them is authentic.*

m.d.　Oh yes, absolutely. They were, really, tremendously kind. They did the cooking for us, made the coffee.

x.g.　*Like in the film.*

m.d.　Yes, yes, they kept house. I know that one day Jeanne ended up making seventeen pots of coffee. It was her record, she said. That happened very, very naturally. I must say that I almost always hire the same crew. The technicians are like my brothers; I've made four films with them.

x.g.　*And how does it work? Everyone reads the script?*

m.d.　Yes. We talk a lot about the script together. For *Jaune le soleil,* there were genuine debates among the actors, Samy Frey, Dionys Mascolo, Catherine Sellers.

x.g.　*. . . who didn't see things the way you did?*

m.d.　Right. And who said that they needed to have certain points clarified, and I always listen to everything, of course. Do you know, I film my movies in eleven or twelve days. The longest was *Détruire,* that was fourteen days. So doing that is worse than . . . no not worse; it's like being in a war . . . you can't imagine what it can be like, the harassed and passionate state you're in at the end.

X.G. *A state of tension. But that's all you do, night and day?*

M.D. Yes. I can see, for *La Femme du Gange,* that the photography director and I were hallucinating from fatigue at the end; we were . . . and so were the actors. [*Silence.*] I'm still very close to the photography director. [*Telephone interruption.*]

M.D. Yes, I'll always make films like that, I think, impoverished films.

X.G. *Impoverished . . . you mean poor in terms of budget?*

M.D. Yes.

X.G. *From the standpoint of plot as well.*

M.D. Yes.

X.G. *Pared-down films?*

M.D. With very few shots.

X.G. *What happens for you when you move from writing to film?*

M.D. Earlier, I think I told you it was to avoid anxiety, fear; I think that's partly why I made films . . . But now it's happening again with films; it's the same thing. You must admit that it's a rotten state to be in, a state like that.

X.G. *But you aren't alone with a film. It takes teamwork.*

M.D. Yes, but for *La Femme du Gange,* for example, the main part of the film was really done in the editing. The image has hardly any substance, but the voices correspond to a crisis as agonizing as . . . the ones I'd discovered in writing—as if those two voices came out of another film.

X.G. *The voices that you spoke?*

M.D. No, that I didn't speak, that I grafted onto each other, that I stuck onto each other; the image film—what I call the image film—is like a bi-film.

X.G. *And you wrote the text for the voices afterward?*

M.D. Yes, yes, when it was completely finished, when the image was completely edited; those voices would just never have made it near the film if the film had been full of images, if the film hadn't had any fissures, any . . . what I call holes, if it hadn't been impoverished—well, that for me is wealth. The poorest films for me

59

are the ones that have two thousand shots. The ones you can only leave feeling depressed, after seeing so much effort, so much labor, so much money laid out to end up with this asphyxiation—nothing more can get in—everything's made explicit, like that.

X.G.   *Everything's blocked up, then.*

M.D.   Everything's blocked up, asphyxiating.

X.G.   *Yes, I really understand that, but the voices don't come to block up the holes in the film either.*

M.D.   No, but they make me think of birds that move between rocks, you know; the voice film makes me think of masses of rock like that in the water, in the sea; the voices move between the masses . . . and they disappear, they come back, they circulate like that between the [*the following word, "waves" (flots) is replaced in the transcription by* îlots] small islands.[27]

X.G.   *Perhaps, they resonate over the waves. At certain moments, you feel almost a clash between the image—well, the image, but I haven't seen it; the description of the image, but it's not a description either . . . the saying of the image . . .*

M.D.   The reading of the image.

X.G.   *Yes, the reading of the image and the voice. At certain moments it collides, it ricochets.*

M.D.   There's a place where the voice film touches the image film. I say "voice film"—a film is an image and a sound. It's for lack of another term that I say "voice film." Yes, there's a shock. They touch each other, and it's fatal. It's fatal, and the voices disappear. So, the conjunction of the films was something dangerous, very dangerous to handle. The death of one or the other of the films was constantly . . . was a constant risk, and I was aware of this danger; that's the reason I did it; it further increases the fragility—fragility, that's not it; I'd say rather the sparseness of the image film, its barren and *minimal* side, as we say today.

X.G.   *But, the fatal moment when the shock happens, that's still something . . . that you can . . . only do alone. Because if it's with the voices that the shock happened and that was death, then you were*

*the voices. That is, you're more alone than in a film crew, aren't
you?*

M.D. Oh yes, all this happened during that night of editing, the kind of
editing night that's extraordinarily fertile. But at the point when
nothing more was possible for the image. I can't forget that. The
image was edited; it's as if I had some free time in front of me, you
see, suddenly, and the voices came at that moment, when I was
relieved of the real work of editing. So they spoke in all directions
and . . . like birds, these voices are birds, it's like a sound of wings.
They speak in all directions. I also had to . . . choose, from all that
they were saying.

X.G. *You had to eliminate?*

M.D. Yes, but that's another film. I can see the film, right now.

X.G. *For example, you just said birds, and you had also said they were
little girls.*

M.D. Girls who are seventeen or eighteen years old. For me, they inhabit
the garret of the hotel, the blockhouse of the closed-down hotel, that
blind upper floor where you can see out only through fanlights, but
very far. They're eighteen years old; they're in rags, in white.
They've been eighteen years old for a very long time, all the time.
They lie in wait for everything. They survey the space. These are
just details. Everyone can see them differently. There's only one way
not to see them, and that's to see them through commentary,
because a commentary would mean a voice outside the film.
Whereas these voices are inside the film. They inhabit the sands,
like the heroes . . . excuse me, like the . . . the people in *La Femme
du Gange;* they live there.

X.G. *In point of fact, a commentary is something that explains, and thus
comes* over *and seals up all the openings there are in the film.*

M.D. That's right. This is the opposite of a commentary, yes, because the
commentary plugs up the holes, while in this case, the voices travel
through the film. They make even more holes in the film. These
voices really overwhelmed me because all of a sudden, the people
who have . . . people who entered into the film, too, many of them

because they saw a great potential there for film . . . I remember at Digne there were a hundred and fifty young people and everyone agreed about this. Which means that you can still do lots and lots of new things with film, use it . . . not to do new things, I'm saying this badly; I mean you can make an *other* cinema; you can use cinema in a way it's never been used before.

x.g. *Yes, when you get right down to it, it's completely aberrant when you think about it, that film is so servile . . .*

m.d. It doesn't budge.

x.g. *It imitates, it retells, it recounts.*

m.d. But there's nothing that imitates itself like cinema.

x.g. *Right, even though there's every possibility in it. I've always been amazed myself that it's so pedestrian, so much the same all the time.*

m.d. Right now the films that younger people are making are all the same. There are series of them like that, which is sad. It's a new kind of brightly colored realism in the New York style, you see.

x.g. *There's a hardness in your films, like an asceticism that's a little . . . because to prune . . . it's to prune a whole encumbering baggage, and to prune is to cut, maybe.*

m.d. Yes, I think that some shots are missing—it's not that they're missing, because often I film them and later I ignore them—what I call transition shots, the intermediary shots.

x.g. *That's it, they're cut; they're taken out.*

m.d. They're taken out, the shots that allow the viewer to move from one sequence to another.

x.g. *To orient themselves, to follow.*

m.d. Is that upsetting?

x.g. *Oh no—well, it is upsetting . . . it means that the bed . . . um, the film is harder—I don't know how to say it; hard, that's not a value judgment—is stronger . . . isn't easy, that's what, there's no facility. One has to admit that there's a facility in most films: that is, when you go to the movies, you're happy; you enter completely into the story; you follow the image and you're happy.*

62

M.D. You're carried along.

X.G. *You're carried along, you're fascinated, you're inside, that's that. That's how it works.*

M.D. Ah yes, that's what I object to, the film's relation to the viewer, in general.

X.G. *A relation of entire passivity.*

M.D. As in Balzac. Everything's digested. You lead him to it—he swallows or he vomits it up, like me; I can't go to them at all anymore.

X.G. *And what's odd is that people have realized for some time that it's no longer possible to write Balzac, but in film, they're still repeating it.*

M.D. Absolutely. Maybe it's because they follow writing. I write in *Nathalie Granger,* for example, when the woman goes to get the newspaper, the letter, and the notebooks, I write "picks up the paper"; next line, "rips it up"; next line, "still rips it up." This is an example. I don't write, "takes three steps, picks it up, straightens, looks at and then tears up the paper and once . . ." Do you see? So it's "picks up the paper"; next line, "rips it up"—there's nothing in between. So maybe because this follows on itself, it's maybe not altogether cinematic writing. But is there a cinematic writing? Who can pride oneself on it?

X.G. *But because until now, cinematic writing has been the most common and the most narrative . . .*

M.D. There is in cinema an enormous pretentiousness, in the world of cinema, that doesn't exist in the literary world, I must say. In cinema, you find . . . the least little guy who's made a film tells you, "This is cinema. Cinema isn't that, this is what it is." And in general, they tell me, "What you do isn't cinema." So then I ask, "What is cinema?" They say, "It's something else, it should move more."—"So the cinema par excellence is the film . . . the Western? That's where things move the most." Then they tell me, "You haven't understood cinema. That's not what we mean." And when I say that a word moves as much as an arm or that a gaze moves as much as a horse, that a shift in gaze is worth the moving of a machine, they don't understand.

x.G.   *But in your films, it's precisely that everything revolves around the gaze. It's fixed, but all space slides and shifts around that gaze.*

m.D.   Yes, in *La Femme du Gange* the gaze does the filming, I can say that. Because usually the gaze . . . one looks and then one sees the object being looked at. But in this case, very often, you have to guess at the object. The gaze is like . . . it's as if one were seeing the work of a camera, through the eyes. You don't see what's being seen.

x.G.   *No, it's not designated.*

m.D.   And the camera never replaces the gaze. The camera films it, it looks at it, it gazes at the gaze, but it can't replace it. That's why my films are so sparse; it's because the gaze always has to be there. You see, if I were a commercial director, I would have shown a multitude of images in *La Femme du Gange:* empty villas, hillsides full of houses, sands, piers, ports, the port of Le Havre, the oil wells of Le Havre, and so on, the refineries. But there's nothing at all, since I show only what is seen. All the rest was made, but I took it all out. There were twelve houses initially, but there are no more than two, two that are seen . . . no, three, three.

x.G.   *So you don't allow the viewer to . . .*
       [End of tape.]

x.G.   *. . . that your films don't allow the reader to enter into the illusion of reality; that is, these aren't realistic films in the sense of the imitation of nature, imitators of life, I mean in the Balzacian sense: a competition in civil status.*

m.D.   No, they aren't like that, except maybe *La Musica.*

x.G.   *Yes, that is still, a little.*

m.D.   But there's some realism in *Nathalie Granger,* isn't there? That is, that realism, too, if pushed to the limit becomes unreal.

x.G.   *Yes, but I don't mean . . . These films are entirely real, but I mean realistic in the sense of pretending to copy reality. I don't know, it's not easy to say. That is, when the woman wipes the table . . .*

M.D.   Yes, I was thinking of the same sequence. Yes. Wipes the table, does the dishes, wipes the dishes . . .

X.G.   *Yes, but, I don't know, there's a way . . . it's filmed so that it doesn't copy reality; it says something about it.*

M.D.   Don't you think that it's just this insistence that means . . . that loses the realistic meaning?

X.G.   *The insistence? You mean the tediousness?*

M.D.   The tediousness.

X.G.   *Well, what people would call tediousness.*

M.D.   The table is shown empty, cleared off; it's shown just as it is. I don't say, "She clears off the table" in the script; I say, "Their hands clear away." And I say at the end, I move to the next line and I say, "The table is cleared." And afterward, we see the cleared table for a long time, while we hear noises in the kitchen; they *must* be in the kitchen. But *we* are still at the table, still glued to the table, whereas *they* are already in the kitchen. There's something strange about that, you see; do you remember?

X.G.   *Yes, yes, I remember.*

M.D.   Maybe it's this discrepancy, it's maybe that instead of showing them . . . the women, clearing off the table, I show the table cleared off.

X.G.   *Yes, yes, that would be it.*

M.D.   That's what demolishes the realism there.

X.G.   *Yes, the women have a kind of . . . of freedom; they're doing something during that time.*

M.D.   That's what it is, but it's interesting, and when we get back to them, we're late. I could have filmed this backwards; I could have preceded them into the kitchen . . . that's what would be done . . . that's what is usually done. So then, the women would have put the camera in the kitchen, and I would have waited for them to come with the last glass, the glasses and the forks. Whereas what I did was to remain with the cleared-off table; what's going on there? These are rather humble discoveries actually. Because I know that I decided it should be this way. In the first version of the script it was already written this way, without my . . . knowing why. I can't explain it to you clearly.

X.G.   *I can't explain it clearly either, but I think that's what the little . . . the little rupture is with what could have been—well, little, but which unleashes everything—with what could have been the copy of reality. But I think that if one can discover, all of a sudden . . .*

M.D.   Realism, because reality—the table also is in reality, alone.

X.G.   *Yes, but the way it's filmed, after the women have left, for example, that doesn't imitate reality; that doesn't copy it, really.*

M.D.   But who sees the table at that point?

X.G.   *I have a feeling it's left to itself.*

M.D.   Right. You could say, "It's the camera." But it's not. The camera's there because the table's there. It stays there as if overcome by weariness. It stays, in front of the table, foolishly, you might say— yes, foolishly. The table takes into account something else, a whole, life . . . Maybe—no, that's a wrong direction—I was going to say life . . . a life at a lower level, a life that's even more . . . even more . . . physical, you see, of the house. In the same way you see the radio, at a certain moment, alone on a table; there's sunshine on it.

X.G.   *Left to itself. But I just think that after having seen the film, lots of people can figure out what woman's work is, what housewives do, what women do in the home anyway. But why? There's something about it . . . For example, if it had been a documentary, like some you see, the factory women, or this or that kind of woman, with that particular realism that documentary films have—I don't know, it would have come across like a news report. But as it is, it's not a news report precisely because of the writing of the film; it's . . . it's something that's happening.*

M.D.   But don't you think we should get back to that notion of realism . . . of *a contrario* realism? Realism would be to show a table when it has a function in the fiction of the film . . . the function of keeping the women busy, all right, but where you jump into unreality is when you show the table all alone, when the women have left.

X.G. *Yes, but I still don't think that's unreality.*

M.D. Oh, I do. It gives me a feeling of unreality; that naked table is magic. There, all of a sudden, the table has a life in itself, a life a little . . . disturbing . . .

X.G. *But . . . well, maybe I don't understand what you're saying . . .*

M.D. . . . competing with the woman. It's the objects touched by the woman and that have their own life. Maybe that's what it is; maybe what I'm saying is stupid, but that's just how it is.

X.G. *No, no, there . . . when you say . . . yes . . . a life, on account of the women having touched it, yes; what frightened me, for a minute when you said . . .*

M.D. Magic?

X.G. *Yes.*

M.D. When I say magic, I mean cinema in general, let's say a cinematographic life, if you like. Because that's what cinema is, oddly enough. You put a camera there, and nothing's happening apparently, but in cinema, it's fantastic; someone's going to come out of that alley and . . . and we'll be frightened.

X.G. *So it reveals, things and people?*

M.D. Yes, and it's not always what you expected; it's always different.

X.G. *Are you the one who does the filming? Are you the one looking into the camera?*

M.D. I always look at the shot, the frame before, before they film, always; and usually, when there are filming mistakes, I keep them. For example, people always talk about this table, which is, in my opinion, one of the essential shots of the film, which gives the tone to everything else, you might say, the mode for filming. Lucia Bose made a mistake in handling the objects on the table; she wasn't supposed to take the glasses first. She made a mistake, she took the glasses; she let them go, she took the silverware. I signaled the photography director to keep shooting. You see how . . . the translation of the mistake is that Lucia Bose is like someone disabled because of her anxiety, and her gestures are completely different from her friend's. They're much more inept, much heavier. Lucky that there was that mistake. But when you take women's work— that's something I'd like to talk about, women's work in the home— how do you see it?

X.G. *I don't know. I see it . . . All right, usually, for me, it's something I can't stand. Fine. It pains me to see a woman cooking for her husband, for example; I'm very ill at ease. It seems like subservience to me, quite crudely. And I assure you that in* Nathalie Granger, *I felt that it was a real labor. Usually, I don't feel that it's a labor that produces anything.*

M.D. In contrast to the notion of chore.

X.G. *Yes, and I got the impression, because of the creation in the house and of the house, that something was going on. And usually, I don't get the impression that it's something that's happening.*

M.D. Right, it's inscribed in a general movement there, in *Nathalie Granger,* isn't it? That's what you mean, that it's a harmonious activity.

X.G. *Yes, yes.*

M.D. Like a movement. As if they were walking.

X.G. *Yes, an activity of their bodies. And that's something I had never realized.*

M.D. Yes, now that you say it, I see that.

X.G. *But what was it in your mind?*

M.D. It was time, the passage of time: they eat, the children leave for school, the husband goes away, they telephone, there are the two or three small chores, they clear the table, they wash the dishes, the dishes are put away, and then presto . . . there's emptiness, free time; the women have two or three hours in front of them, empty, like that.

X.G. *I wonder if time for a man is the same as for a woman. That's probably absurd, put that way.*

M.D. It's the same in prisons. I've often read descriptions of prisons from people who had been in prison; they enumerate the same way: they're brought their tray, they eat, mouthful by mouthful—time

68

passes, you see—they put down the tray, someone knocks, they give back the tray, and presto . . . there's free time. It's only in prisons that man lives woman's experience of time, lives it, I think, completely. Because this kind of activity—I can see it spaced out there right at this moment—this activity is completely unknown by men, completely. For them, it goes without saying. It's not even work. It's like an eating-away, like an intestinal, glandular labor. They don't see it as any more than that.

x.g. *That goes along with what I was saying, that this doesn't exist as labor.*

m.d. For men, woman is so predisposed to it that . . . she dissolves within it.

x.g. *Yes, it forms part of her.*

m.d. But if you ask lots of women what they do, women from low-cost housing and all that and even in the bourgeoisie, what they do in the afternoons, they say that's the problem; if there's boredom, that's where it is, during those hours. This hole in the afternoon, between chores and the arrival of the children or the husband . . . It's almost a suicidal tendency.

x.g. *When outside violence bursts in . . . at different moments when more or less violent intrusions from the outside strike these women, isn't there a time change then? Maybe an acceleration of time? Is time the same for the Yveline criminals . . .*

m.d. No.

x.g. *. . . and these two women?*

m.d. The intrusion of violence disturbs even the flow of time. The intrusion introduces another duration, which relates to a longer duration for women, you see. What's touched upon at the women's houses at that moment goes much further than the women on that afternoon. It's what these women have been forever, probably. But to come back to the issue of work: I don't see anything man does as being on the level of household chores. Most of them have jobs, of course, but different ones, whereas 95 or 98 percent of the world's women have the same job.

X.G.   *It's strange, because I wonder . . . it should bring them together, you would think, it should provide them . . .*

M.D.   Yes, but it's totally hidden, and women don't even talk about it anymore. It's like breathing.

X.G.   *Yes, again, it's not a job.*

M.D.   In my film, is it a job?

X.G.   *Yes, for the first time.*

M.D.   When you say "job," it means that it's not degraded, right?

X.G.   *Not at all.*

M.D.   Right, it's revalorized, basically.

X.G.   *All right, it would be . . . This might be a little removed, what I'm going to say, but let's say for example, if you think about labor in the Marxist sense . . .*

M.D.   Yes, exactly, I wanted to get to that.

X.G.   *. . . it's a production of something, which is useful to society, which is remunerated in exchange, and which makes society function, really. But women's work in society is a different story, since it's not recognized as work, it's not remunerated, and in spite of everything it supports the men who work; it maintains their strength to work. For example, women wash their clothes; women feed them. So, why is there that framework?*

M.D.   There's a kind of break there, a complete break.

X.G.   *Yes. Why does it have . . .*

M.D.   Because it's not paid. Because it's not in the cycle of production.

X.G.   *Of course it's not, but still . . .*

M.D.   Either it's playful, or else it's chores. Everything that's not paid is either holidays or chores . . . well, household chores . . . That's what women's work is.

X.G.   *Exactly, chores, even in the sense of the serfs, really; that is, they didn't get paid and their life . . . In exchange for that, the women have a life . . . well, so-called . . .*

M.D.   But if you analyze a woman's life, it's very, very . . . the life is extremely contained, that is, the relation, the exchange. Women don't have that whole . . . they don't have that enormous advantage—the woman who doesn't do anything—the enormous advantage of work, of a workplace, for communication, which man's workplace represents.

X.G. *Of course, but see, you too said, "The woman who doesn't do anything," which is to say the one who works at home, but . . .*

M.D. Right.

X.G. *And then, they don't consider women to be doing anything inside the home, actually, since they're not working outside of it.*

M.D. "Who don't earn wages," we should say.

X.G. *She's not a wage-earner; she's kept.*

M.D. But it's so much inside of us. How . . . how can . . . It's not that . . . that the woman would have to be outside, handed over to the outside, like the man. That's not the problem, in my opinion . . . really, the problem, is . . . the major problem, as I see it, is how to keep a woman from cleaning a dirty table, how to keep a woman from doing the dishes when the dishes are dirty, how to keep a woman from feeding a child when he's hungry.

X.G. *It would be an incredible crime not to do it.*

M.D. And do you think we'd have to get to the point where we wouldn't do it?

X.G. *I don't know. No, I don't see why systematically chasing women away from what they've always done and—still, on the other hand, it's a problem that they repeat the way they do. I don't know.*

M.D. When you see a man do household tasks, it's so difficult, so pitiful; you feel like telling him, "Let me do it."

X.G. *For that matter, I think they do it badly so that we'll say, "Listen, you're not getting it . . ." Well . . . maybe unconsciously there's a kind of messing up that way.*

M.D. A man sewing on a button is really pathetic.

X.G. *Still, maybe as far as that goes, we might be in a transition period now too, don't you think? After all, it's true that as little girls we were taught to sew on buttons.*

M.D. Look how in small towns where the children do the shopping, it's the little girls who do it. The mother sends the little girl because she already knows that the little girl won't lose the money as often as the boy would and that she'll know better how to say the items to the grocer and butcher. And so that's how it is.

x.g.   *But that's how it is . . . I don't know . . .*

m.d.   I mean, they say it naturally; it doesn't occur to them to . . .

x.g.   *Yes, it seems natural, but isn't it because, from the beginning . . .*

m.d.   Oh, of course, because they've been raised that way.

x.g.   *Yes, because if they send the little boy, first of all, he's going to be made fun of: "What! You're doing the marketing!" Well, I don't know . . . It's such a part of the machine, from the beginning; there's just a kind of shame that he'd feel doing housework, which* could *be transformed into its opposite, pride; "I do the housework at my house!" or something like that. But it just never seems to work out that way.*

m.d.   But then, this work, when maidservants[28] or cleaning women do it, do you judge it on the same grounds?

x.g.   *That's a problem for me too, but at least they have a wage.*

m.d.   Women who simply *are* and who have a wage. I think of the women at the beginning of the century, a great courtesan who'd be kept, and then of the women of today, women on the Boulevard Haussman, kept by . . . businessmen. They're paid . . .

x.g.   *Yes, but it's not a wage.*

m.d.   They have apartments . . .

x.g.   *Yes, but it's not a wage.*

m.d.   They're given money . . .

x.g.   *It's not the same thing.*

m.d.   . . . cars, furs . . . I see that as a wage.

x.g.   *No, I don't think it's a wage. They're kept; in exchange for being the woman, they're given money. A wage is in exchange for work.*[29]

m.d.   But all of bourgeois society, married women, who have domestic servants, who do nothing . . .[30]

x.g.   *Yes, it's based on that.*

m.d.   They're kept women?

x.g.   *Yes.*

M.D. And the fact of being kept, is it . . . well, I find it intolerable.

X.G. *Of course, it's disastrous.*

M.D. Intolerable, intolerable.

X.G. *Completely disastrous.*

M.D. And do you think that women of the bourgeoisie are aware of this now?

X.G. *I don't know—a little, yes, since it seems that there are more who work a bit.*

M.D. You find fewer and fewer women who let themselves be supported that way, completely, by the husband, whereas twenty years ago still, it was considered totally normal and even desirable. All parents wanted this for their daughters.

X.G. *Yes, yes, even though if the wife works, it's something extra. It's when she doesn't have young children, it's when . . . in order to fill up her life a little bit, it can be part-time work. It's not the same conception of work.*

M.D. To alleviate her boredom.

X.G. *Yes. So as not to be the idle woman of leisure anymore, and in fact . . . if their work isn't necessary, it's not real work either.*

M.D. Yes, exactly.

X.G. *After all, if they get tired of it, they stop. It's not the same for a man's job.*

M.D. . . . or work done by women in poor circumstances, in working-class milieus . . . who run the boat. Each house is like a boat, and the women are in the machine room, down below. Without this, everything would stop.

X.G. *Yes, but usually those women do a double job.*

M.D. Usually they do double. We could talk about boredom, if you want, the boredom of these women.

X.G. *Do you have the impression that the women in the film, in* Nathalie Granger, *are bored? When they're listening to the traveling salesman, for example?*

M.D. No, no.

X.G. *They live quite well, I think.*

M.D. Lots of people have asked me that, after seeing the film, and I've always answered, "No, they're not bored."

X.G. *They feel good, I think.*

M.D. Well, there's the problem of the child.

X.G. *Yes, the child who by no means accepts their rhythm either, their women's time.*

M.D. And who's against . . . against everything; that is, at school, she's against the teacher, against everything that's proposed.

X.G. *Yes, she's in revolt, absolutely.*

M.D. Absolutely. It's a formless violence but extremely painful, and this violence weighs down all the sky in the park; it weighs down the whole house. What should be done with the child? What should be done with the child in view of society? These are both intolerable, you see, the intolerableness of the child and of society. What do you do with a child once you've created it? I believe that right now, everywhere in the world, all pregnancy is dramatic. People talk about India. An Indian woman's pregnancy is necessarily a drama. She asks herself, "Will my child be able to eat? Is he going to live for three years even?" Okay, but it's the same here, too. Everywhere in the West, in America, what's a child going to become? What will his future be in this horrible society?

X.G. *Personally, I can't imagine how you can raise a child.*

M.D. It's not possible. I think people propose that as a principle. They have children so as not to be bored; they propose it as a goal because they no longer have anything else. Life within the group has ceased completely; village and community life has ended. People are bored to death; this cry is everywhere, boredom; nothing happens anymore. So, they give themselves a child, just like that. They make a child in order to give themselves a . . . not even a goal—that would be saying too much.

X.G. *A front.*

M.D. That's it, or an occupation, I would say. And when a child has a room, that's luck; when he has a place in school, that's luck; when he finds a job, that's very lucky. As far as this goes, we could go back to the passivity we were talking about and make more of it. Everything's in keeping with it. It's very odd how in this world this process turns up everywhere: in cars and children. People have a car, but they don't know where to put it; it's the same.

x.g. *Yes, they have a child; they don't know where to put it.*

m.d. Exactly. You have a car, you get punished. You get tickets because you have a car. You have a child, you get punished; they don't give you a place for him at school, and they all rave, "Have children and buy our cars!" It's a circle that way, a vicious one that surrounds the individual. Everywhere. In all areas. You're told, "Go on vacation!" There's no place for you on vacation. There's no room at all. It's altogether too expensive. The least house is six hundred thousand francs per month, and they tell you: "Go ahead, get it!"

x.g. *But what can we do? Do we have to refuse everything?*

m.d. We have to—I don't know, it's . . . it's a thing we've never tried. Besides that, there's the vote . . .

x.g. *Yes, that! what a fraud.*

m.d. Exactly. And that's where passivity should have gone to work immediately. You try to find someone to vote for: there's no one. Even if you say "no," you open the dialogue. That was what the Gaullist referenda were, that huge, huge intellectual fraud. "Tell me if you choose me . . ." And you felt like telling him, "But we haven't asked you for anything." Everybody toed the line. And well, I think, you see, that we wouldn't have toed the line that way before, fifty, a hundred years ago. I think people are getting more stupid. They aren't aware of where it . . . of where things don't fit, where the thing is . . . invalid, when the demand is invalid, that it's a false demand.

x.g. *And you think they were aware of this before?*

m.d. I think there was more intelligence; I've got that impression.

x.g. *You can make people believe more things maybe, make them believe that they're intelligent, for example.*

m.d. Yes. No, but it seems to me that a man who's very, very, very simple who's told "Choose me"—I'm talking about the vote, I mean, on all levels, the electoral vote, the referendum—it seems that this very simple man would realize immediately that he hadn't asked for anything and he should ask, "But why should I choose you? I don't choose anyone. I'd rather choose someone else who doesn't ask me anything." The real stupidity is to toe the line.

X.G. *Yes. They keep making people believe that they're free. And that in voting, for example, they're saying something.*

M.D. Yes. But it's amazing how effective that is.

X.G. *But there are more means of propaganda and brainwashing these days.*

M.D. Yes.

X.G. *And the more they stupefy people, the more they tell them, "Look . . . ," they explain to them, "Look, you're free, you're intelligent, you can choose, you can do that," but it's mostly because they're told, I think.*

M.D. But the people who denounce lots of things are demanding to move to political action, when the first thing to do would be to abstain. Tell people above all, before the programs, "Don't pay your phone bill, rob department stores, don't buy any more cars, don't vote anymore, don't pay your taxes." But if only there were millions doing it.

X.G. *But that's the problem.*

M.D. That's the whole thing. I dream of an entirely negative political program like that.[31]

X.G. *Actually, people kind of want something like that, but at the same time there's a superego and a law that crushes them, I think. I heard about a . . . about a group in the U.S., young politicized people . . . I don't really know what they are. They go into the huge supermarkets, you know, where there's sometimes a person who demonstrates items with a little mike to say, "Buy Super Product X," all that. They come along and take hold of the guy, they shove him aside, and they take the mike and say, "For half an hour, you can take everything you want; it's absolutely free."*

76

M.D. And no one takes anything? Or do they?

X.G. *It seems that everyone rushes to it . . .*

M.D. Because the first time nobody dared to.

X.G. *. . . from what I've been told.*

M.D. At first, people didn't dare budge.

X.G. *Yes, it might have been like that too. It seems that they did this and that people rushed in . . . well, after several times . . . they repeat their announcement; they say it again . . . they rush in to steal. So, all right, this is a crazy feeling for people . . .*

M.D. In America, they have silent politics like that—or gestural, rather— which is perfect, which was perfect during the Vietnam War.

X.G. *It was?*

M.D. Refusing to pay taxes—there was a widespread refusal to pay the phone bill, especially in the state of New York.

X.G. *Yes.*

M.D. But we're in the kind of situation . . . well, we mustn't . . . this isn't an interview necessarily about an era, this or that era . . . well, what I mean is just that the inertia, the refusals, passive refusals, the refusal to respond, basically, is a colossal strength; it's the strength of the child, for example, the strength of the woman.

X.G. *Yes.*

M.D. It's a kind of feminine strength, which doesn't explain itself, this refusal, and I think women could oppose with it. Men would always go immediately to discourse in order to explain, wouldn't they, to make it explicit. But women could oppose it. They would *feel* it immediately, and I think that they would *act* if they had speech. Unfortunately, as things are, in 95 percent of the cases, everybody just follows along.

X.G. *But that's because we've also got this splitting up of women . . . It's pretty strange because, it's as you were saying, they almost all do the same work, but each in her own house or apartment, but men who have different jobs meet in the workplace and have something like that in common even if it's artificial.*

M.D. That's what public life is.

X.G. *And that's why it's difficult to . . . Why doesn't this women's passive refusal come about?*

M.D. Because it corresponds . . . it might be that we have to go back to Marxism . . . it's not a Marxist kind of work. It's not a kind of work that can be politically fruitful. It's not collective; it's isolated.

X.G. *Yes, that's true.*

M.D. Maybe it isn't because it's unpaid but rather because it's isolated. Each woman in her kitchen, each in her box, doing the same thing. Suppose there were collective kitchens, village kitchens or village laundries, things would be totally different. If a whole village lived in a single dormitory, things would be totally different. Women's work would become . . . would have political consequences.

X.G. *Yes, but even then there might be another problem: that is, when a man goes on strike, he doesn't do it alone; he's got a whole organization against his boss, his employer. If a woman goes on strike in some way—refuses to get up, for example—her boss is her husband or her lover, some man with whom she has affective, sexual relations, and so on; it's much more difficult.*

M.D. In any case, that can't be a strike; it won't be looked on as a strike by the man.

X.G. *That's right. It's very different.*

M.D. I think that the person-to-person relationship is rarely a consciously political relationship. That has to be impersonal. You've got a political relationship between a boss and a worker who don't know each other, who are connected by the wage given and the wage received. But in a couple, obviously, even though it's eminently desirable, the relation can never be . . . I don't think that it can ever become political. I think that it's women among themselves who should . . . who should group together and . . . act. Not the woman in her home, but the woman outside her home.

X.G. *But the problem is precisely that they have contradictory interests, affective and sexual interests. It's that, if they do something among themselves, they each have a husband or a man who will oppose it*

78

and who will hold them back by this affectivity, by everything, by relations that are entirely subjective.

M.D. Well, then, we shouldn't live with them.

X.G. *With men?*

M.D. Right.

X.G. *That's a problem too.*

M.D. We should have lovers, husbands maybe, but we shouldn't live together . . . that is, lay ourselves open to that, lay ourselves open to subservience. Which comes immediately.

X.G. *Yes. And you think that we can have lovers or husbands without entering into an affective relationship?*

M.D. Oh, there will be an affective relation. There'll be . . . but this way there won't be the taking over of the husband's upkeep and of the house on the part of the woman. Because she'd have her own place, and the husband would have his too. It's the place in common that has to be broken up, maybe. The household, that is.

X.G. *It's strange because, look, with* Nathalie Granger *you started off with a house that saved women, in a way . . . well, saved them not in the Christian sense, but it was really security, a harbor, for the women . . .*

M.D. They're not overburdened with work; it's been surmounted, you understand. The work has been surmounted there because it's infrequent, it's . . . the women have . . .

X.G. *Yes, but aren't they as isolated as other women?*

M.D. Yes, they're isolated.

X.G. *If they stay in their house, can they do anything? And afterward, you say—we're getting to that now—you say, "The house must be broken."*

M.D. Yes, but it's . . . the house in *Nathalie Granger* is a house that breaks in the end; it's broken, it's destroyed.

X.G. *It opens up.*

M.D. Everybody enters it. It's opened and it's on account of this small accident that the little girl won't go to school anymore—we don't know what will become of her—that the house breaks apart. In the chain, it's just the link that's missing, the little girl, socially dislodged, that makes everything else break apart . . . The house opens up. Oh no, I could never have made a film where the house would close up. My house is always open.

X.G. *Yes, that's true.*

M.D. You've noticed?

X.G. *Of course.*

M.D. Right now, the front door's open. If we go to the front door, since we're in the same house, we might find a traveling salesman.

X.G. *Yes . . .*

M.D. I close it at night. Or when I'm all alone.

X.G. *Besides, it's really open; well . . . it's not just the door, or the door latch; it's that it's true that people come here and . . . are at home somehow; that's what the openness is.*

M.D. Yes. It's because I don't live with anyone.

X.G. *That's true, yes.*

M.D. A few years ago I met a man who wanted to live with me and who said, "The first thing we'll do is to close ourselves up at N—"; no one will come there anymore, live there anymore. What a horrible, horrible thought!

X.G. *Well, that brings up the question of the couple again. Is a couple two people in a closed place?*

M.D. It's a closed economy that has consequences for . . . the existence of the couple has total consequences as far as . . . the impact of the couple on the individual is total. It goes to the depths of the individual. When a man and a woman are a couple, nothing about them is ever quite the same as before, nothing; everything changes. Everything.[32] It's incredible. They're one in two. The couples that get along, that work out. I don't remember where I talked about that.

X.G. *Is this desirable?*

M.D. I don't think so. I've got the very clear, even luminous impression now that it's since I've stopped living with a man that I've completely found myself again. All my books, the ones you're talking about, that count for you—I wrote them without a man, or else with men just passing through, who didn't count; they were passing adventures, which are the opposite of the couple. Just the kind that you avoid in coupled life.

X.G. *What you're saying is really important.*

M.D. You can really see . . . it seems to me that you can read this through the books . . . that they're books of solitude.

X.G. *But in your books, there are no couples. There are passions between people but never a couple, two people, that is.*

M.D. The couple is horrible, people who say to each other, "We're going to move in together": "move in together" is a popular expression . . . which says exactly what it means.[33] To eat the same thing, in the same space, to close doors.

X.G. *It's . . . it's a way to keep warm, to feel reassured.*

M.D. Oh yes, it's to avoid adventure completely. The only valuable thing is adventure; I'm not talking about adventures of love and passion but any adventure—of the spirit, anything.

X.G. *Yes, and in spite of everything I've got the feeling that it's especially the woman that it refuses the . . .*
     [End of tape.]

M.D. . . . whom they say are closely linked, they are . . . they are, relatively speaking they are, the ones who are on our side politically, completely open to a revolutionary necessity, anyway . . . and who say, in all innocence, "Without my wife, I'd never be who I am." And when you ask them, "And what about her?" they don't understand.

X.G. *It's crazy.*

M.D. The worst thing in this system of thinking—I heard it recently in connection with music, with women and music. I was saying that just as the working class hasn't begun to compose, neither have women. There's no woman composer because, to compose music, the individual has to be totally free. It's an activity—how can I say it?—the man who takes himself for God isn't . . . the one in the legend is really the musician. A man has to be in total possession of his freedom to come to music. That's what I was saying, and someone retorted, "Woman doesn't need to create music, because she *is* music!"

X.G.   *And man plays her . . . as he plays music.*

M.D.   Man profits from her.

X.G.   *Yes, but in both senses.*

M.D.   Right, and this came as a huge compliment from this friend. The sentence began, "You don't understand—you don't need to create music, you are music."

X.G.   *And then, when people say that to women, they're flattered.*

M.D.   Yes, the women who were there seemed thrilled. And when I howled, they must have said to themselves, "There she goes with her bad temper . . . always contradicting . . ."

Fourth Interview

X.G.   *What do you think?*

M.D.   Fine.

X.G.   *Otherwise, we might have a hard time going back to using the formal pronoun.*[34] [Silence.] *I don't know. No, I don't know. Begin if you like. Go ahead.*

M.D.   "Isn't aware of being looked at," yes: is what strikes you the . . . is it the negative? It's that you'd usually say, maybe, "People are looking at her, she doesn't know it."

X.G.   *Yes, do you realize the number of personal pronouns, yes, personal pronouns and . . . that that adds!*

M.D.   I had noticed that, that usually you watch something being done or else you watch something being undone. You look at the fullness. Not the hollowness. Yes. "Doesn't see that they're looking at her" is something that, for me, is done just as much as "sees that they're looking at her." This distraction is more important. You almost always know that you're being looked at. [*Silence.*]

X.G.   *Yes.*

M.D.   Well, there you are.

X.G.   *This leads us right to* La Femme du Gange, *because the whole film is made that way.*

M.D.   Yes.

X.G.   *Isn't it?*

M.D.   That's right—last time you hadn't seen it.

x.g.   *No.*

m.d.   You had read the script.

x.g.   *When we began? No, I hadn't read anything. Because the whole film is made like that, through the hollow gaze. [Long silence.]*

m.d.   The mini-cassette is running. [*Laughter.*]

m.d.   If only we could keep the silence in the typography . . .

x.g.   *Yes, I know. It doesn't matter. It'll come out. [Silence.] No, but I don't know, I'm afraid to speak about it, about* La Femme du Gange. *Especially, I don't want it to be filled in, you see, for it to be a . . . for us to say things about it to . . . to fill in the film, you see, with all the exits it has, all the hollows it has . . .*[35]

m.d.   At first there's a breaking up of the whole, even so. Of three books. [*Silence.*] It's continually being undone and then it's redone as . . . as it can . . . that is, I make mistakes, but I keep them.

x.g.   *You make mistakes . . .*

m.d.   In the chronology. I don't know anymore what happened in the books.

x.g.   *You only keep what's essential. I mean what's striking, what struck you.*

m.d.   I've just reread *Le Vice-consul;* I had completely forgotten that they had already been in India for a long time, Anne-Marie Stretter and Michael Richardson. I had completely forgotten. It's because there's a real hollowness that's available there. Yesterday I got a phone call; someone said to me, "It's really interesting how you devised things"—how did they say it again?—"organized." I said that I hadn't organized anything at all. This person tried to see explanations everywhere.

x.g.   *But that's what I'm afraid of, you see.*

m.d.   Explanations in details. She thought that the woman dressed in black in *La Femme du Gange* was another Lol. V. Stein. In my opinion, she's not; in my opinion, she's Tatiana Karl. So she said to me, "But she does such and such . . . and in the books Tatiana Karl doesn't do that." I said, "But I have forgotten my books. And when I do something like that, I do it as much with a forgetfulness of my

84

books—a false recollection,[36] I mean—as with a recollection of them." The two go together. I know that now. In a way, it bothers me a little to have reread *Le Vice-consul,* because I'm doing something with it now . . . well, something that has to do with what's silenced in *Le Vice-consul,* you see . . . There are things not said in *Le Vice-consul,* and that would be the subject of . . . of a . . . something to come.[37]

X.G. *But there's always something that—well, I don't know, in what you will do—well, it's certain . . . there will also be something that will be silenced, which can be said—it's indefinite, infinite, I mean. It . . . it . . . there's always a hollow structure that's waiting, that can wait for something.*

M.D. Yes, but why does it always turn around those two . . . places: Nepal, and the North, the West, an empty place, S. Thala? Why? Why? Nepal, I still think, is childhood. It's not possible, it's not possible, for it to exert such a fascination over me. I saw Calcutta once, but I was seventeen years old. I spent a day there—it was a port of call—and that, I never forgot. And leprosy is something I saw at Singapore, on the Singapore customs wharf.[38] I've never forgotten. But I think I've got to go further back than Calcutta and Singapore. Have to go to . . . to the ricefields in the south of Indochina.

X.G. *Where you'd been?*

M.D. Where I was born.

X.G. *That would be going backwards somewhat. Because . . . well no, not in* Le Vice-consul, *but for example in* La Femme du Gange—*ah, not there either, it's odd—I was trying to find some order in the beach on the Atlantic and the heat. Anyway, in* Lol. V. Stein, *it's the call toward something else; it goes in the opposite direction from what you lived yourself.*[39]

M.D. *Lol. V. Stein* already dates from my adult period.

X.G. *But it goes in the opposite direction.*

M.D. Yes.

X.G. *She's in the North and there's someone who leaves to go up there.*

> *But you did the opposite. As if she were going—for example, when Richardson goes away, as if he were going toward a past, so then, toward your past.*

M.D. Yes, yes, that's true.

X.G. *And in* La Femme du Gange, *that's also a past.*

M.D. It's a universal past, everybody's past, isn't it? When she says, "Any past is what I remember," she dies of remembering. I believe it's a common past. It's *the* past.[40]

X.G. *But their . . . memory, their desires, are also common.*

M.D. Yes.

X.G. *I mean, they're just as much ours as theirs, since they don't have them anymore. All four of them—the madman, the young man, Lol. V. Stein, and then the woman in black too—have gotten to the point where they no longer have anything of their own. They say as much. Neither their desire, nor their memory—none of it belongs to them.*

M.D. It's a state, yes. The refusal was as if it was done by generations who preceded, the refusal of society. Don't you think so?

X.G. *Yes.*

M.D. They're not the ones who brought it about. It's that infamous book again that we were talking about, which was blocked out: the passage from fullness to emptiness, which I never wrote.

X.G. *Yes, but, for example, for the traveler it hasn't happened yet. The film is this passage.*

M.D. It's in process, that's true. That's what it is; the film is this passage, exactly.

X.G. *It gives him a passage.*

M.D. He joins them.

X.G. *For example, since he came to kill himself, it was still a very personal desire; he really believed that he could kill himself. Whereas the others . . . he doesn't need to kill himself after all; the others make him come into this . . . into this place where they're already dead, where in some sense it's already happened.*

M.D. It's the same. This state of refusal is the same; it could be taken for a state of death. But in fact, on the contrary, it's a state of birth, isn't it?

x.g. *Yes.*

m.d. But he kills himself in a way that's extremely . . . widespread. I think that . . . it's impossible to see society in place around oneself, to *see* it—all right, it's rare that one sees; there's maybe one person in a hundred who sees—without feeling like committing suicide. Their ugly faces on television, that makes you want to kill yourself.

x.g. *Yes, but still, to kill oneself, as you might think the traveler did with his . . .*

[Telephone interruption.]

x.g. *I don't remember what we were saying.*

m.d. Do you want to play back the last part for me?

x.g. *Yes. I think I was trying to say that when you see him on the bed, as if he were dead, with the medicine, it seems to me that that's still a moment when . . . he could still ask himself what it is to die. You understand?*

m.d. Yes.

x.g. *So he's still in a life, one that's relatively banal, because when you're in a life like that, you say, "I want to die." Then later, it's no longer possible . . .*

m.d. It's the last time he asks himself that, maybe.

x.g. *Yes, yes, it seems that way to me. And afterward, when he's completely taken by them, there's no reason to ask himself that anymore; there's no longer any . . . I don't know how to say it . . .*

m.d. There's no longer any preferential act, you could say.

x.g. *Yes, yes.*

m.d. Because to kill yourself is still a preferential act. That's what's hateful about suicide. Fortunately, it's available to us, because life would be totally, totally, totally unlivable if it weren't available; but it's still a preferential act.

x.g. *It's an act of will.*

m.d. Right.

X.G.   *Whereas afterward, that's no longer a question, I think; he can no longer think that he can or that he must do something.*[41]

M.D.   An equivalence is produced. He joins them, and it's as if he had killed himself—except that he's alive, and that is his refusal. If he were dead, there would be no refusal. We can refuse. This passivity, this immense force that the mad people of S. Thala have, this organic refusal,[42] if you will, can only be exerted in life. He kills himself to a certain order of things; he dies to a certain order of things, to what is proposed. But me too—I died to that order of things. You too. In our milieu you see only people who have died . . . to the *rest*.

X.G.   *Yes.*

M.D.   So, this traveler is right there with us. Okay, what happens afterward—that is, that he recognized that girl as being Lol. V. Stein, the girl he killed—but he never gives in to guilt, to remorse . . .

X.G.   *That doesn't make sense anymore, either, does it?*

M.D.   No.

X.G.   *Guilt would mean that he willed that act, that he wanted to kill her.*

M.D.   Exactly, exactly.

X.G.   *Whereas he didn't want to. It happened.*

M.D.   It happened within the force of their desire, when the lovers left the ball. They didn't see anything anymore; they didn't hear anything anymore. She called to them because she wanted to follow them right then, but the call was completely futile.[43] She called to them, moreover, because they'd gotten to the point where they could no longer hear anything. It's true. That's what she is, Lol. V. Stein, this kind of equilibrium in disequilibrium. It's what I've called the three terms of desire, the desire between the lovers and the desire Lol. V. Stein has to join them. But the distance between her and the lovers was insurmountable.

X.G.   *It was insurmountable and yet it was very, very . . . it existed. It's like a link. It's an insurmountable distance, but it's like a link.*

M.D.   That's it, it's this distance she didn't surmount that ties her to them, that ties *her* to them . . .

X.G.   *Yes.*

M.D.   . . . to the point . . . where she becomes mentally ill.

X.G.   *And that's why, finally, she follows anything at all . . . like the madman. It's not the lovers anymore; she follows anything that moves. So it was still almost too personal [a desire] when she was following the lovers, yet this could take another form, through the madman.*

M.D.   It takes a debased form, it takes the debased form that it has in life, don't you think?

X.G.   *Yes, in fact, but don't you believe that in life people think they know they're following a very specific person, without realizing that what they're following is where desire is, where love is?*

M.D.   Yes, the person is a momentary prop. Is that what you mean?

X.G.   *That's it.*

M.D.   Yes, from the beginning it is always the same love, displaced from person to person.

X.G.   *Yes, in your film, that's what it is.*

M.D.   Yes. But when you see a child play, a young child who plays in a really basic way, he takes a piece of grass, a pebble; he looks at it. All right, this state of play for the child—in view of a later time when he'll have toys made for playing, toys made by adults—you have the same debasement in play. The child is a completely mad creature who becomes subdued. And in *L'Amour*, in any case, in *Lol. V. Stein*, it's absolutely what you've just said. You said that the madman . . . wait . . . what did you say about the madman in connection with the lovers?

X.G.   *He takes their place for Lol. V. Stein; that is, instead of following the lovers, she follows the madman, but it's the same thing. It's not that he is the lovers, but he has the same value for her.*

M.D.   That's it, but should the lovers present themselves, she couldn't . . . she'd follow them just as she follows the madman. She is destroyed.

89

X.G. *But at the end, she follows the traveler.*

M.D. She was really destroyed during the night of S. Thala. Yes, she follows the traveler.

X.G. *So, in a certain way, you could believe that she finds him again, that he was the one she was supposed to follow from the beginning, but then again, it's not even him, I think.*

M.D. Right, in my mind, that's the most desperate moment.

X.G. *Yes, it's really frightening.*

M.D. When she begins to follow the traveler, as she followed the madman, without any realization, that's when it's over. Hope is really . . .

X.G. *That's it.*

M.D. . . . pulled out by the roots.

X.G. *Exactly, because then he would be the one she wanted to follow from the beginning, but when she follows him, it's just the same as when she followed the madman.*

M.D. It is said, "She follows whatever moves, whatever goes."

X.G. *Yes.*

M.D. Right, the form remains; that's what it is.[44]

X.G. *Yes. But . . . what moves, exactly, all . . . the movement in* La Femme du Gange . . . *You see, that's maybe what is most impressive, the way the movement is at the same time a slowness . . . actually, it's more than just slow, it's slowed down, slow motion— relative to what, I don't know; maybe to what we're used to seeing, or slowed down in connection to what it "should" be, in . . .*

M.D. But didn't you feel that way because it's always the same pace? It's not that the pace is particularly slow; it's that it's always the same, so then you think it's slowed down. Usually, in films, they go faster in certain places and slower in others. There's never any urgency here.

X.G. *Yes. And it's the same. You say, "It's the same pace"; that is, you can move from one character to another. It's the same thing for desire. But by slowed down, I mean . . . yes, maybe because sometimes you see accelerations . . .*

M.D. But not in the film?

X.G. *No, not in the film. You usually see accelerations, but there aren't any here. And, you see, the desire and the pain are so strong . . . you could imagine freeing yourself from them by making a quicker movement, or by taking a quicker step. That's why I say "slowed down." And it's . . . for me, that's what eroticism is. I felt it in a very, very erotic way . . . a slowed-down movement, I don't know how to say it any other way. That is, the tension is so strong, it rises so high, yet there's no quick gesture or step that would discharge it, that would attain a goal.*

M.D. Orgasm?

X.G. *Yes, orgasm.*

M.D. That's it, there's no orgasm.

X.G. *That's what it is, and that's why it's an unbearable eroticism; you almost need for it to go faster and it doesn't go faster, so it's . . . you feel it all the more strongly, you see . . . and then . . . at the same time, there's the movement, then, that I've called slowed down and yet at certain moments there is—not a rapidity but a blazing. For example, when the woman sings, with her mouth closed, moving her head, it's incredible.*

M.D. She sings slowly. There's more intensity, further intensity in her voice. The sound is stronger, not faster.

X.G. *The rhythm is the same. It's not faster. It's blazing.*

M.D. They walk the way she speaks.

X.G. *Yes, it's the same rhythm. And yet, there, it rips open.*

M.D. Notice that there was this same pace in *Nathalie Granger*, wasn't there? Maybe there were still some differences.

X.G. *It's true that* Nathalie Granger *is more incorporated in a social reality.*

M.D. Yes, you see, the young people of Digne—where the film was seen, after all, by a hundred and fifty people—they brought this to the organizers' attention; they told them, "You wanted to make us believe that *Nathalie Granger* was a 'different' film, a different film-vision. It's not true at all. The film-vision that's different is *La Femme du Gange.*" What do you think of that?

X.G. I *think that it's already in* Nathalie Granger, *this different vision, but that it's complete—that is, there's a* totally *different kind in* La Femme du Gange.

M.D. Yes, but in *La Femme du Gange,* from the standpoint of the viewer's entry into the film, of—that's what it is, the viewer's integration in the film—in *Nathalie Granger,* you can like it a little, you can like certain things, you can more or less not enter it. Enter more or less into the film, I mean.

X.G. *Yes, yes, I understand.*

M.D. Whereas in *La Femme du Gange,* if you don't enter into it, there's nothing there.

X.G. *It's all or nothing, right.*

M.D. Nothing at all.

X.G. *Yes. And we can discuss* Nathalie Granger *more, I think, than* La Femme du Gange, *which . . . is complete, for me, which completely overwhelmed me.*

M.D. That's right. Just as you can get into it to a greater or lesser degree, you can speak about it to a greater or lesser degree.[45]

X.G. *Yes. And you see—I hadn't thought about* that *while reading the script—when I heard the married woman speak, the woman with children, the social woman, in the script . . .*

M.D. Now she, you see—I interrupted, excuse me—she walks faster; *she's not from S. Thala.*

X.G. *That's certainly clear.*

M.D. She's from the sixteenth district.

X.G. *And her voice!*

M.D. She has Pompidou as her tutor.

X.G. *Yes indeed, you can sense that right away.*

M.D. She's rotten, she's a lost cause. And she walks quickly in S. Thala, which is shocking.

X.G. *Yes, it's true. When I saw them, the woman and the two children, I said to myself—I don't remember this in the script—it was as if there'd been an error in the shooting, as if you'd caught people walking in front of the camera by mistake, who were real people, you see, people who weren't in the film. I swear that at one point I said to myself, "But who are those people? It can't be that she just caught them in the camera." I didn't remember who that woman was.*

M.D. Yes, but people like . . . the influential commercial directors would say, "Now, *that's* cinema."

X.G. *Exactly, they'd feel safe with that.*

M.D. So, she comes down. She comes down, she charges down; afterward she walks faster; she's frightened, so she cries; she's sad, so she cries, and so on.

X.G. *Yes, it's logical. What I meant is that when I heard her speak, I said to myself, "Maybe she could be the viewer as well . . ."*

M.D. Yes, like Gélin, in *Détruire*, who is the viewer.

X.G. *Because, for example, when she says, "But really, I don't under-stand; what does it mean? I'd like an explanation. I have the right to one, I think," I thought I was hearing a viewer in the room saying, "But really, what is this film? I've got the right to an explanation!"*

M.D. As a matter of fact, I thought about that; you're absolutely correct. I laughed during the filming and I laughed while writing it. And I thought it was something a viewer would say.

X.G. *That's it, one who would say, "It seems to me I have a right to an explanation," that is, someone who's utterly lost. And also when she asks, "How long has this been going on?" and when he tells her, "Forever," that's about the film, too.*

M.D. Yes, and he says, "I didn't know that."

X.G. *He says, "I've only known it for a while"—and we only know it when we see it; that's what the film is. But it's been going on forever, yes.*

M.D. You see, when I talk about an accident of memory, I could just as well talk about indecision in vision, a vision that's not totally determined. The dead ball at S. Thala, I see it just as well in the hall of the hotel—the Roches Noires Hotel in Trouville, which is like a

93

blockhouse—as in the municipal Casino. So I filmed both. It's a glaring contradiction.

x.g. *In theory, yes.*

m.d. The viewer could tell me, "But where did it take place?" What does it matter? For me, it happened in two places.

x.g. *No, but you see, the film is made out of that, out of what the viewer could say about contradictions, whether in place or in time, it's the same thing. At what moment did something happen? It happened, it happens again, it comes back, it'll happen in the future too, I think.*

m.d. That's just about what Michèle said.

x.g. *Yes, it's true that the film starts over, is going to start over.*

m.d. But Blanchot, talking about *Détruire*, said something to me that amused me and yet struck me at the same time; he said, "You have to give it nonstop. That is, put a touch of black at the end of the film and then start over with the first image." And I thought he was kidding, but he was serious.

x.g. *Yes, of course. And that's what Blanchot says when he talks about writing. He says, it's something that can't stop, and that's his sickness, basically, the writer's, that he can't stop—it can't stop and gets said constantly. I think in telling you that . . . it's what real writing is for him. [Silence.] I'm thinking, on the other hand, about the photography, the views of the sea. It's true, too, that the sea doesn't exist like that, you know, when you see it.*

m.d. It's a liquid world.

x.g. *So then, in the film, it begins to take on an existence . . . I remember one shot: the sea is far away, there's sand and banks of sea, banks of water.*

m.d. At dusk?

x.g. *At dusk, and you see it so suddenly it's a shock!*

m.d. Yes, where she says . . . the voice says, "Do you sometimes feel like dying?" Gold and blue. I must say that I had a cameraman, who's also one of my friends, who was really heroic. Absolutely no other cameraman would have filmed that, those night shots. He would have felt humiliated. But I'm happy for him because the director of

94

the New York film festival who's just requested the film—which
makes me happy, by the way—said to me, "I don't remember—who
is your photography director?—I don't remember ever having seen a
shot as beautiful as that." I'll have to call him, my friend, to tell him
that . . .

X.G. *Yes, at times, the scenes are out of this world.*

M.D. It's like being in mourning for color, don't you think? I made it and
he made it with me—Bruno Nuytten is his name. He's a guy who
didn't . . . we did it both together, really we were plunged into
mourning because we had to put in some color; we were sad, and
that comes across.

X.G. *Yes, it's a very, very particular color. It's not at all a color that gives
color . . .*

M.D. That's right, that's quite correct.

X.G. *The films are . . . they're slightly colored, you know, the way
children color: there's an outline drawn and they color the inside.
But this is the complete opposite, and it's true that by comparison
other films appear colored.[46] It's a whole, an entirety, what you see;
the color and what is said are indiscernible.*

M.D. It has a different function than in other films. Why do they use color
usually in films?—what I'm going to say isn't mean; I really believe
it—it's there to help the rest go down, to help the viewer eat the food
of the film. You see these things on dishes in restaurants, colored
things, pieces of radishes, flowers sometimes. It's to help the food go
down. Because people tell themselves that maybe the material being
presented is too poor, too meager to stand alone. Someone told me—
Benoît Jacquot, my assistant for the two films—he said, "It's natural
that *Nathalie Granger,* which doesn't open up to anything, which
stays closed in until the end and which finally opens out onto two
dead axes, two blind axes, two blind holes—it's natural that it's in
black and white, and that the other film, which is about what
Nathalie Granger opens onto, is in color, because at that point it
opens onto a totality, and you take what's there. Color is there, you
take it, the sand is there, you take all that's there." I don't know, but

I felt there was something right about what he was saying.

X.G.   *Yes. Yes, it has to be part of the whole.*

M.D.   They're all in black because it's in color. In white and black.

X.G.   *The clothes of the woman in black are fabulous.*

M.D.   She's extremely beautiful.

X.G.   *With her face completely white. She's a kind of bird of prey. It's as if she's lying in wait.*

M.D.   She surveys the sands.

X.G.   *She's different.*

M.D.   She's not in *L'Amour,* but she's in *Lol. V. Stein.*

X.G.   *Even though she too has lost everything.*

M.D.   She still has a room at the hotel.

X.G.   *Yes, she still has a room; she's different from the three others. She also has a way of questioning and of speaking that's very different . . .*[47]

M.D.   She's indecent.

X.G.   *. . . from that of the madman who does nothing but acquiesce, or from that of Lol. V. Stein who doesn't speak, or from that of the young man who's completely mute, completely.*

M.D.   Yes, they're doubles. That too was an accident in filming. And I'm really happy it happened. Because Gérard Depardieu said to me, "I can't do the film; I've brought you someone else. I have to finish Dominici." *The Dominici Affair.* [*Laughter.*] "I signed an agreement. I can't do anything about it, I have to finish. So I've brought you a young man to replace me." Then, two days later, he showed up himself, saying, "I'll be able to do the film after all." So I kept everything, just as I kept both women in *Nathalie Granger.* Even if three or four actors had turned up, I still would have kept them.

X.G.   *That's what gets into the camera . . .*

M.D.   Yes. You have to leave that. You have to let it happen the way you meet people in the street.

X.G.   *But it's really strange, that young man who's mute, and I was thinking—probably you didn't want it like that—that again it accounted for a kind of reversal, a reversal of the two young girls, whom we never see and who speak through the whole film; but him we see a lot, and he never speaks.*[48]

M.D. He says a "yes"—"Is he crazy?" "Yes"—once. I was the one who said it for him, by the way, in the dubbing.

X.G. *Oh, really? That was your voice?*

M.D. The voices are dubbed, the *voice-ons*. I really like them; it's as if they're stuck on.

X.G. *They seem a bit foreign to the . . .*

M.D. Yes, I really like that. I can't stand the realistic tone of films anymore. But if you like, we can come back to that Ganges we were speaking about, to that excuse for a place in Calcutta, that kind of melting pot; everything comes from there.

X.G. *Yes.*

M.D. The sands there in S. Thala, that's Tonle-Sap, where the beggar woman comes from. Don't you think that's childhood?

X.G. *Yes.*

M.D. The forest in *Détruire* is childhood.

X.G. *Yes, like a place . . . where one could have begun to live.*

M.D. Perhaps that's only where I have lived. Maybe I've been under a suspended sentence since I've been in France, in this rotted, rotten fatherland. You know, back there, we lived without politeness, with no manners, with no fixed hours, barefoot. I spoke Vietnamese. My earliest games were to go into the forest with my brothers. I don't know, there must be something inalterable that remains after that.

X.G. *But isn't it also—not only for you, you see—the resurgence of a culture more ancient than Western culture, which has policed everything, which has rounded off all the hard edges and put things in place?*

M.D. Ah, it would be nice if it were . . .

X.G. *A culture that's stronger, you see, more generous. There's a kind of generosity.*

M.D. You think that this can just get deposited in a little . . . white girl, passing through.

X.G. *Yes, absolutely, even though this runs counter, let me remind you, to*

97

what you were saying the other day.[49]

M.D. But no, that doesn't run counter to it, because there was a double language. I was bilingual. I took my *bac*[50] in Vietnamese.

X.G. *But maybe just because of that, it allowed you, who also had another culture, to feel that culture as something . . . like a past now, but also something strange and stronger that comes to shake up Western civilization a bit. People who are entirely in one or the other can't feel that.*

M.D. And yet they do feel it; otherwise, no one would understand me. If I feel it and other people agree, they feel it too. So we all have it in us. It's not just me.

X.G. *Yes, yes.*

M.D. It's the same, for the viewer or the author.

X.G. *I mean that you were able to say it in a very particular way— because after all, it's you who said it—maybe because you had this double culture*[51] *that everybody has, you see, like something one can wait for, hope for, imagine; but you—you lived it. That's why we can be open to it. We couldn't live otherwise.*

M.D. By means of my extradition here.

X.G. *Yes.*

M.D. You know, my mother ruined herself because of the dam. I've told the story.[52] I was eighteen when I left to take the second part of my *philo* here and to go to the university, and I didn't think about childhood anymore. It had been too painful. I completely blocked it out. And I dragged along in life saying: *I* have no native country; I don't recognize anything around me here, but the country where I lived is atrocious. It had colonialism and all that, right?

X.G. *Yes, it did.*

M.D. And I think this is revenge for that. The native country has avenged itself.

X.G. *It resurfaced all the more violently because of having been suppressed.*

M.D. I was twelve years old. We had a house in Sadec, on the Mekong.

Okay. I remember a colonial administrator. He's dead, but his kids might still be living. His name was B——. And in Indochina at that time there was a tax, a kind of per capita tax, for peasants and inhabitants, and at the time when this tax was to be paid—I've seen this, I saw this for years, every year at the same time—multitudes of junks came down from the countrysides (the Mekong irrigates thousands of kilometers, as you know) in their small boats, in their sampans; these people, lots and lots of these people, brought their tax to the administrator. But that's all they had, the three or ten piastres—I don't remember anymore—folded in a handkerchief. Whatever. When they got to the office of the colonial administration, of the general administrator (since that's what it's called), they were told, "Ah yes, that will be three piastres (or ten) plus one piastre for the administrator." Many of them didn't have that one piastre, and they would stay for days and nights waiting along the Mekong, all those clusters of boats, and my mother pointed them out to me and said, "Look, they're waiting, they don't have the piastre for B——."[53] All right, I've tried to forget that. That was a different time. My mother told me the prices; luckily, she told me everything. A Legion of Honor medal cost eighteen thousand piastres. So it was the biggest crooks in Indochina who had the Legion of Honor. But to get back to this Mekong, full of countless boats, it was marvelous to see, the black sampans, you know; the Mekong is extremely muddy during the rainy season. I blocked out everything, because B—— . . . I couldn't stand him. I told myself, "If I hold on to this knowledge all the time, it will kill me. It could kill me, so I have to cut it out." But the Mekong still remained somewhere. This Mekong next to which I slept, played, lived for ten years of my life, it stayed with me. Then when I say, "What is that murmuring? It's the Ganges," it's the Mekong speaking. Do you see? Near the dam, the Whites, those bastards, built a station called Bokor. They had it built by convicts, Vietnamese convicts. The convicts were people who, for example, couldn't pay the tax. So the whole road was—my mother told me all about it—the whole road was like the Way of the Cross. Every kilometer, every two kilometers, you could see holes filled up with people who'd been put there to force them to work, to punish them; they were put in the ground up to their necks, under the sun, as an example. Okay, I blocked out Bokor. But Bokor was part of the Elephant Chain where I used to go with my brother during siesta to kill monkeys. That was horrible; one killed whatever one found. And it was there that I had the greatest frights in my life, because my brother would stop and say to me, "Listen to the tiger." We would hear the tiger. We would see birds slaughtered by the tigers—I told about this in *Le Barrage*. And the enormous creepers above our heads were full of fish. We used to wonder where the fish came from, thirty meters above us in the jungle. These were creepers that had accumulated over the centuries, you understand [*end of the tape*] [and that had formed basins suspended between the trees].

M.D.　Yes, well, it was incredible. We'd try to climb up, but we couldn't; we were ten years old, twelve years old. I guess I'm telling you about these basins because I have a bedazzled memory of them, don't I? Of the night like that in the forest, during the night, under the basins—it was incredible, when we'd walk underneath, barefoot, barefoot while everywhere it was teeming with snakes! . . . Well, enough of that. My mother would sleep during that time. So I blocked all that out because of Bokor. But the forest—I find it again everywhere. And to be perfectly frank, I'm always afraid. I have never once in my life been able to go five hundred meters in a forest by myself without being terrified.

X.G.　*But at the time, you weren't afraid at all.*

M.D.　Not at all. The things we did, we should have died twenty-five times over.

X.G.　*It's funny, because you might see this also as an omission, as if you hadn't lived the fear when you should have lived it.*

M.D.　Yes, that's obvious. And it's what you're in the middle of telling me, what I'm telling you. I wasn't afraid at twelve, and then, as an adult,

I've thought about it a lot and said to myself, "But how did we get out alive?" We would go to the mouth of the *rac*[54] to see the monkeys, I swear, and there were black panthers, too. I saw a black panther fly by a hundred meters away. Nothing in the world is more ferocious than that. I used to go on sampans—with my brother, always—they were chock-full of caimans. We used to catch the little ones and eat them.

x.g.   *Ahhh! Did you cook them?*

m.d.   No, they were in brine. We were so poor we ate anything, birds, seabirds that stunk of fish. Well, I told about this, though not completely, in *Le Barrage*. Obviously, in *Le Barrage,* I didn't want to tell everything. I wanted it to be harmonious. I'd been told, "It has to be harmonious." It was much later that I moved on to incoherence.

x.g.   *But, you know, now that you tell me this, I also can see* La Femme du Gange *as a revenge against colonialism; that is, that there, in Trouville, on the cold beach, the Ganges empties; Asia surges up . . .*

m.d.   It's the mouth of the river.

x.g.   *. . . you see, Asia invades . . . invades this West . . .*

m.d.   Ah, that's right.

x.g.   *. . . instead of Whites who invaded Indochina, you see, there's a kind of reversal.*[55]

m.d.   Yes, but when you talk about passion, nobody loves anyone anymore at S. Thala. They're bathed in desire, but it's nonpreferential, as we were saying. But don't you also agree (this goes back to what you were saying) that passion in the Stendhalian sense, or, if you like, Balzacian, Proustian—let's go as far as that—is lived in the past? When she speaks about the past celebrations in S. Thala, when she says, "What a love it was; when I think of what it has been . . ." isn't that a class society? Because in class society there is something to miss, in everything, in everything there's something to miss. There's something to miss in class society too. Don't you think it's a world crazy with exasperation about love that is over? In my mind, it is over.[56]

X.G.   *It's also the scraps, then, of a world . . . of the world . . . of the world where we still are.*

M.D.   Yes, passion will come back, but for the moment it's like a reprieve. Maybe . . .

X.G.   *What you're saying is important, but it can always link up, I think, with . . .*

M.D.   . . . colonialism.

X.G.   *. . . Asian culture and Western culture. Because I'm not very familiar with Asian culture, but I know what the West is like, and what we get from Descartes—but passing through Stendhal and others—is this illusion that we're masters of ourselves and that we have an ego and that we're the ones who desire, and so on. And in other cultures, in Islamic culture, for example—in Balinese culture, too; I know, because I've been to Bali—and I think also in Asian culture, they don't have this illusion. People aren't kept within this "philosophy" of the West, and there's a tremendous submission to what they call . . . well, that depends . . . destiny or whatever, but it means something that's stronger than we are and that travels through us. Do you see what I mean?*

M.D.   Yes, but it's in us. It's stronger than we are, but since we create it, it's in us. There's something in us that's stronger than we are.

X.G.   *Yes, it's in us. Fine. For some cultures, it's externalized; they say, "It's . . ."*

M.D.   "It's God."

X.G.   *Exactly, right. That's an illusion, too. But they have nevertheless understood, much more than Westerners, that it was stronger than we are. Whereas Westerners always believe that they're the ones who create and who think. Fine—"the thinking reed" and this monstrous joke we live in.*

M.D.   But Kant said something really idiotic about it.

X.G.   *They all said idiotic things.*

M.D.   Kant said that in order for man to progress, he would have to have a superman as a model. That's one of the stupidest things anyone can say.

X.G.   *Yes, yes.*

M.D.   So then this superman, since man thought him up, is inside himself. And what does it mean anyway? What a horrible word!

X.G.   *Well, all right, in your film, all that is completely swept aside, and couldn't that also come from Asian culture, which is different?*

M.D.   Obviously, I'm incapable of telling you. For me, it was just as serious as if I'd been a little Vietnamese girl. I've got memories[57] . . . ah . . . more beautiful than anything I will ever be able to write. The seashore—what's that called . . . it's the Gulf of . . . I don't remember—where we used to go on vacation, always, with my brother; we used to get lost in the mountains . . . we'd see Buddhist monasteries, small isolated pagodas, the calm there; the men there had this exceptional calm, this absence from themselves, you see.[58]

X.G.   *Exactly . . .*

M.D.   In the midst of tigers, of all kinds of dangers, malaria, dysentery. Yes, those men—I never saw them again.

X.G.   *Is there guilt in that culture, as there is for Christians?*

M.D.   Oh, not at all!

X.G.   *Ah, you see.*

M.D.   That's what's shocking.

X.G.   *But there, too, it's because Christians think that they're masters of themselves, and so when they commit a sin, they have to redeem themselves.*

M.D.   Exactly.

X.G.   *It's awful.*

M.D.   Guilt—that again comes out of megalomania, out of pride.

X.G.   *Yes, really; are you aware of everything your film knocks down?*

M.D.   It's what Sartre too drags along with him. The same thing. Whereas I don't have either the intellectual's or the writer's guilt.

X.G.   *His philosophy is inherited straight from that, from Western philosophy.*

M.D.   Well, the girls I knew back there—all my girlfriends were Vietnamese—up to the age of sixteen had a kind of joy, a *joie de vivre* that was very primitive.

X.G. *We don't know what that is here.*

M.D. No. I was going to say something horrible: it's as if the state of being a young lady had never been achieved. Well, that's a horrible thing because young lady, in this context, is a degraded term, a pejorative term. I remember a grace, almost a collective grace, you see, that circulated among these young girls that was . . . that came out of a kind of receptivity to nature. They spoke little; they had a good time among themselves, and they welcomed the rain, the heat, the fruit they ate, swimming in the rivers—you see, it was apparently a very, very, very basic receptivity.

X.G. *That's how it is in Bali. It makes me think of Bali, what you've just said. They have a real community life.*

M.D. There's that gentleness, and then an absence of all feeling of jealousy among the girls, or of sadness. There was no sadness, no preoccupation with knowing how they were going to live, what they would do. They were my mother's students. Some whom she took in were very poor.

X.G. *But the education your mother gave them—well, this isn't a criticism of your mother—wasn't it a Western education?*

M.D. It was absurd. She used to laugh about it herself sometimes. Yes, she used to say sometimes, I remember, "Joan of Arc, what's that supposed to mean to them?" [*Laughter.*]

X.G. *But I think that—this might seem a bit unconnected, but I think it's very much tied in—class society is the same; it's very different but the process, the Marxist approach, is also a complete sweeping aside. Man is no longer what he believed himself to be, with Marxist analysis.*

M.D. Every man is informed of Marxism. Isn't that what you mean?

X.G. *Every man is what?*

M.D. . . . is informed about Marxism.

X.G. *I don't understand what you mean.*

M.D. He knows what Marxism is these days.

X.G. *Yes, but what I also mean is that, in Marxism, you know that you've been determined in a certain way, by economic forms, by economic and social relations.*

M.D. That's right, each man is in a chain of production, and he knows it.

X.G. *It's also a way of realizing that man is not at the head, as he thought he was, you see—at the head of something, in charge of what he says, of what he thinks.*

M.D. Yes, but you have to take Marxism as a momentary, direct analysis of reality.

X.G. *Yes, but don't you think that in that sense it can be used against all Western philosophy?*

M.D. What?

X.G. *Marxism.*

M.D. That it would run counter to all Western philosophy? . . . which is rationalism, basically. No, what do you call that philosophy that makes man master of himself?

X.G. *No . . .*

M.D. All essentialist philosophies, then.

X.G. *Yes, but all Western philosophy is like that; it's the philosophy of the "ego," you know, the "I think" of Descartes; that's the premise. And the Marxist subject can't say "I think" like that, since he knows he thinks because of one thing or another.*

M.D. No, he has to deflect the conjugation: "I would think like that if . . ."

X.G. *Yes, but don't you think . . . You see why I say this, how this connects to the work that you are doing?*

M.D. Hmmm? . . . Yes, to destroy this illusion of man as Marxism destroys it . . .

X.G. *Yes, in a different way.*

M.D. The illusion that man determines himself.

X.G. *Yes, of the man-God.*

M.D. But Marxists know themselves to be overdetermined, determined from the outside—I don't know if they say "overdetermined"—by the process of production. But my people . . .

X.G. *. . . it's from the inside?*

M.D. They don't *know* anymore; it's the word "know" that's shocking.

X.G. *Yes, I really understand. I can't say at all that it's the same. In a certain way, they've gotten further with it, your people.*

M.D. Yes, you could say: either it wasn't worth it for them to go through that stage or else that they went through it a hundred years ago.

X.G. *Yes, that's it.*

M.D. But they come out of Marxism in the sense that they're everybody.

X.G. *Yes.*

M.D. They conduct themselves in terms of refusal in the same way, all of them, whatever they may be. The same way that the man who has a Marxist consciousness[59] can infinitely reproduce himself; that's what's called the proletariat. Yes, that's Marxist.

X.G. *They've gotten to a place where there's no . . . I don't know how to say it; the word's rather offensive—but where there's no boss.*

M.D. But I'm also talking about what they think of themselves as such. They don't think of themselves in terms like "I, Paul Durand, I'm escaping . . ."

X.G. *No, absolutely not. We're talking about the same thing, you know.*

M.D. But I don't know whether the egalitarian function that's at play here can be called Marxism or passivity.

X.G. *Passivity, of course. But I don't want to call it Marxism at all, you know. I just wanted to say . . . that there was a process here that was very politically correct.*

M.D. Yes. We can come back to that. Passivity, I'll talk about passivity. We agree. But it's *informed* passivity. The passive man informed about reality. So, he's Marxist. When I talk about the passivity that could inaugurate a woman's politics, as a response to the proposition of the class society in its current form, I'm talking about a passivity that's completely informed about itself, completely. Otherwise, there would be nothing; otherwise, it's garbage. You also have to treat Marxism as a kind of knowledge. Because it's really astonishing—I don't know whether we've already spoken about this—I was saying it just now: every man, 90 percent of the proletariat, is informed. I'm talking about the Western proletariat; for immigrants let's say 50 percent, for the European proletariat, here—well, I'm talking about large industrial capitalist nations like Germany, Italy, France—up to

90 percent of the proletariat knows about the law of surplus value and the terms of its exploitation; the worker knows perfectly well the terms of his exploitation. He knows his Marxist equation. Fine. That's not enough to move on to action. Why not? Because he believes he's got to move on to action. And action, at present, is more and more impossible, more and more difficult, more and more ambiguous.[60]

X.G. *There's more and more an acceptance, you mean?*

M.D. Yes. There's a kind of schizophrenic crossing between the proletariat's knowledge and its subjection. I said this to an English journalist, but still I can say it here. All right, it's just like a person who's mentally ill—he knows all about psychoanalysis; he can practically analyze his own case, but the illness remains. His knowledge isn't enough.[61] I think there's a relation between the two, between the general and the particular. It's clear that the research right now—revolutionary research, research about the necessity for revolution—is more concerned with the means than the basis. The basis is completely inventoried. We know everything, everything that's happening to us; we can analyze it, synthesize it. All the books that come out revolve around it. What we're looking for is the way to exploit this knowledge.

X.G. *And then that's where woman's force comes into it.*

M.D. Yes. But there will be idiots who'll tell me that *La Femme du Gange* isn't political, I know it.

X.G. *How absurd!*

M.D. I'm ashamed for people sometimes. When I see how they carried on for Druon,[62] good heavens! How people went so far as to answer to that ass, that zero! Really! . . . To hold a demonstration for that! It's shameful. I really feel embarrassed for them.

X.G. *It's too good for him!*

M.D. Yes. I was also embarrassed when Brezhnev fell into the arms of that Vietnam man, Nixon. You think you're detached and then still you're ashamed. That feeling remains. That's enough. I've talked a lot today.

x.g.   *That's fine. But I'd also like for you to talk about woman's power in your film, because isn't the force of feminine desire, mad desire—madmen and women—the only force left in your film?*

m.d.   Yes.

x.g.   *It's the only one possible now?*

m.d.   Children's, too, when they're not plagiarizing adults. Woman is the force. Socially, madness is not a force because madness can't be organized. It remains outside of Marxism, if you will. I think the force has to be organized.

x.g.   *And women can do it?*

m.d.   Women can do it. If women were listened to, they could. They have to organize this listening so that they can make themselves heard. This great passivity, which seems to me fundamental—it's only women really who can impose it, who can provide the example of it.

x.g.   *But . . .*

m.d.   So they're in a kind of passivity, I would say, that's very important, of course, for their . . . their case. They separate themselves from men; they live in groups; they exist in a kind of passivity in relation to man; they refuse him. But I think that if this passivity could get out of the groups, and if women could get out on the streets and refuse what's proposed, they would live their femininity as much as in a closed group. That's what bothers me, because you can call this whatever you want, I mean, that's not it; you can turn it around for . . . for an hour, but it's still a militancy, to close oneself in among one's own.

x.g.   *Which is when they're together?*

m.d.   Yes.

x.g.   *But the thing is that they really have to . . .*

m.d.   Even in its inside use, it's a kind of militancy.[63] But I think that imposing a force on the outside that they feel is specific to themselves—this refusal, this passivity; there are many more powers they haven't yet fully used—this is a way, a mode of knowing themselves that's as strong as that of . . . maybe stronger . . . more sure, more fruitful than the . . . than exchanging words in a closed group.

X.G. *But . . .*

M.D. I don't say "chatting," because that's pejorative.

X.G. *But to know where their strength is and to find themselves, they still have to be together at a certain point. It's not something isolated. As you were saying before, there have to be individual discoveries, but we need to speak among women, among ourselves . . .*

M.D. Let that be another time, then.

X.G. *. . . we need to speak our body's experiences, for example, as we were saying in the conversation we had the other day here, if you remember. I mean at dinner, with the man. Do you remember that conversation? That discussion?*

M.D. No.

X.G. *. . . It was here, it was really violent! With a man!*

M.D. Oh, yes! The man that was here.

X.G. *Yes. And where you were saying, "The important thing is that we women tell our experiences to one another"—I don't remember, about pregnancy, for example. You were speaking about pregnancy.*

M.D. Yes.

X.G. *Don't you think it's important for you to talk about it to a woman, to me, to Michèle, to Solange, or whoever, and that they talk about it too?*

M.D. No, they were talking about it to someone who was a man . . .

X.G. *But a man was there, and that's just what makes for problems.*

M.D. But still he heard it. Even if he fought like the devil, he heard everything.

X.G. *But don't you think that women have to have times when they speak among themselves? So that they know where they are . . .*

M.D. Yes, well, for me, I can't quite believe that. I think that you find everything on your own. But that's my . . . that's my failing. That's my . . . my sickness. That's how it is. It's my sickness. Maybe I would feel really fine in a circle of women, I don't know.

X.G. *It's not about a circle; it doesn't have to be a circle. No, but I was thinking myself . . .*

M.D. It's obvious that I can talk to you because you're a woman.

X.G. *Well . . . yes, that's what I think, you see.*

M.D. Yes, yes.

X.G. *I think, for example, that between the two of us we say things that we understand, each of us, but that a man . . . it's not that he wouldn't understand, but it would be different.*[64]

M.D. No, he wouldn't understand.

X.G. *He would be elsewhere . . . well, I don't know, it's just some things have to be between women.*

M.D. Yes, but he would understand the refusal, for example . . . Suppose a man goes down a street where a group of women . . . are writing on the walls. That's what we were saying the other day, the ABC's of protest, and its very foundation: "Don't pay your taxes, don't pay your phone bill, don't listen to them anymore, don't answer them anymore." It would be impossible for the man to remain insensitive to this, just impossible.

X.G. *Yes, but he'd become terribly angry.*[65]

M.D. No. First of all, anger, as always with women, the men get angry first; when women write books, men always get angry. But even so, in the end they think it over, and they'll have seen and heard.

X.G. *Yes. That will come. I think it's going to be very slow, you know.*

M.D. Obviously, I'm talking about an act that's public, a word that has an effect on the real, that has an impact. So, it's about a political action but one that's—what's that called, when it's in two parts?—that's double. Woman, making herself, writing on walls, declares herself, and to herself, in a profound way; at the same time, she's declaring herself to the outside. There's a double movement, a conjunction—that's the word I'm looking for.

X.G. *Yes, and there certainly must be both.*

M.D. Maybe. I've never been in a group of women. I don't know. I've always had a kind of . . . personal speech with women. During a whole period of my life I couldn't stand women at all.

X.G.   *Oh, really? And now that's changing?*

M.D.   Oh, yes. I see practically no one but . . . women, or else homosexuals. We have to talk about that.
       [*Telephone interruption.*]

M.D.   I know a lot of women in my position who can tolerate only the homosexual male . . . only men who are homosexual.

X.G.   *That's how it is for me, too, most of the time.*

M.D.   Yes. Maybe it's not even worth explaining, it goes so much without saying.

X.G.   *For me, too, it seems obvious that I can't stand "men" men, the ones who . . . I don't know . . . who attack, who want to . . . to hold us down . . . well, do you see?*

M.D.   That is, they live against a background of despair and fear that opens them up.

X.G.   *Homosexuals, you mean?*

M.D.   Yes, like us.

X.G.   *Yes.*

M.D.   We share something basic—let's say in the oppression by the phallic class. But a man as he was understood twenty years ago, you know, a strong man who builds the future [*laughter*], ah, ah, that's over with. Not one of them gets into my house.

X.G.   *I can't stand it. It makes me laugh, at best.*

M.D.   Are there still men like that among writers?

X.G.   *There are men like that everywhere, but . . . You see, still, it's true that I myself feel much closer to male homosexuals . . .*

M.D.   Wait, we've made a jump. There are no more men like that except in criticism.

X.G.   *Yes.*

M.D.   You know what I mean? All the men in criticism are real men.

X.G.   *Lots and lots of them, yes.*

M.D.   [*Inaudible words.*]

X.G.   *Do you think you should say all of them?*

M.D.   Oh, I don't know; look at the criticism in *Le Monde*.

X.G. *Yes. [Laughter.] Precisely. What's happened . . . No, but I was thinking, I don't know, about people who sometimes do critical texts . . . like S——— or B——— . . . that's still a different kind of criticism.*

M.D. B——— is homosexual.

X.G. *Yes.*

M.D. And S——— is . . . desperate. [*Laughter.*]

X.G. *Yes, that's what I was thinking: it's true that I feel much closer to homosexuals than to other men, but in spite of everything, I feel that we don't have to say either that it's—well, you didn't say it . . . but thinking it's the same thing—that women and homosexuals are in the same place.*

M.D. Oh, no, what I'm saying is that what brings them together, what joins them, is a base of fear and despair, a common base.

X.G. *Yes, yes, I agree completely with that.*

M.D. It's a common lot, one of oppression, there's no doubt about it.

X.G. *But there's . . . okay, the bodies are different, the ways of feeling are still different, right. Pregnancy is something for example, that they can't experience any more than other men.*

M.D. No, never—not even in a distant future! . . .

X.G. *No, of course not. What I mean is, we still have to see what's specific, completely specific to woman, don't we?*

M.D. Yes.

X.G. *What she has that's really hers.*

M.D. What's absolutely, absolutely hers, the very last thing that she has and that men don't have, is pregnancy; that's immutable.

X.G. *Yes indeed.*

M.D. But do you remember when I said to that man, "Can you put yourself in the place of a Black?" he said yes. I answer as a woman, and I say no. "Can you put yourself in the place of a pregnant woman?" He said, "Yes."

X.G. *What nerve!*

M.D. If someone said to me, "Can you put yourself in the place of a man with a phallus?" I'd say no.

x.g. *. . . or one who has problems with it, like the question he raised about an impotent man.*

m.d. Yes. He speaks from the viewpoint of the role he gives himself . . .

x.g. *Yes, but it's always been like that.*

m.d. . . . that of stage manager. It's true that that's not at all tolerable anymore, not at all.

x.g. *Um . . . what's specific to woman is pregnancy and—I know that in general you're not supposed to say the word, but her period is also something that belongs to woman.*

m.d. There is her period.

x.g. *And that's a subject that's completely taboo.*

m.d. It's the same thing.

x.g. *And in spite of everything, it's woman's body, it happens in her body, and men can't know what it is. To know what it's really like for the woman. Women don't have the right to speak about it, because it's really a subject . . . it's considered such a dirty thing. Woman is considered a bit like someone dirty.*

m.d. Yes, really. For teenage boys, a period is always traumatic. It's an excess, an overfullness that's thrown out of the body, rejected by the body, it's . . . yes, that's it.

x.g. *You see, I think it can be really important for women to talk together about this, for example, because usually if it was spoken about at all, it was in whispers . . .*

m.d. It's our mothers who got us used to that. My mother used to tell me, "You mustn't talk about periods or about syphilis."

x.g. *You see, it's considered a shameful sickness to have a period.*

m.d. Yes. "Don't tell anybody," she would say to me.

x.g. *Yes, you'd think it was a sickness we have, and then that we have it every month. But still that's really, really important; I mean, look at the repetition, that we live it so often and it's something that we have to live alone, that society forces us to live alone.*

m.d. Oh, completely alone, like pregnancy. With pregnancy, for a very long time in our society, people hid themselves; women used to hide themselves when they were pregnant even in bourgeois households

and marriages; there was that prejudice that you don't make
death[66] . . . love, excuse me, to a pregnant woman.

x.g. *Nor to a woman with her period; it's the same thing.*

m.d. Yes, it's dirty; it soils.

x.g. *Woman is considered impure; it's an impurity. It's the same in
religion—she's impure.*

m.d. In the Jewish religion.

x.g. *In the Muslim religion also.*

m.d. They can't touch her; what's going on?

x.g. *In the Christian religion, is this kind of thing approved of? I can't
remember anymore what they say.*

m.d. Well, our holy . . . Mary, mother of God, never had a child; she
escaped . . .

x.g. *Oh yes, that was a taint.*

m.d. . . . the chore. So she must not have had periods. Immaculate, what
does that mean?

x.g. *Well, yes, she has no stains.*

m.d. Well, there you have it.

x.g. *At last, a pure woman! The only one! That means all the others are
impure; all the others are maculate.*

m.d. All right, that's an interpretation of nature that was distorted from
the start, because you could also regard periods as a surplus of life,
an excess of life.

x.g. *And it's really part of our life, part of our body; I consider it as
something that's part of me, anyway, and I don't know, it's . . . not
like an illness.*

m.d. Oh, no.

x.g. *But in the beginning it was terrifying for me; it was an illness, an
embarrassment; but it's society that makes us . . . makes us believe
that. You know, I think there's a whole area of work, which may
take a long time, of . . . recognition of woman's body, so that she
discovers herself. When I see advertisements, for example, I've
amused myself by taking note of advertisements in the so-called
women's magazines like* Elle *or* Marie-France, *you know, advertise-*

> *ments about periods, advertisements for tampons! Well, it's just incredible; they write, "A doctor thought of it for you, a gynecologist conceived it, it's made this way so that you'll smell better and so that it's discreet, so no one can see it, it's always that way, and so that you won't smell bad." Really, it's . . . you see, first it's men who think like this, and then it's all so that . . . presumably we talk about it, but precisely so that we don't talk about it, so that it will be all the better hidden, in fact, all the more nonexistent. All the while it exists.*

M.D. Like truth, it's the same thing; upbringing has a lot to do with it. To teach a child not to tell the truth, you codify both lies and truth: "You can do this, you can't do that." I don't see any intrinsic difference.

X.G. *Could I have another cigarette?*

M.D. Of course.

X.G. *All right, but I think back to . . . for example. Lol. V. Stein's passivity. She's become totally passive; she follows; she no longer speaks.*

M.D. From the moment that she could no longer follow the lovers.

X.G. *Yes.*

M.D. Do you agree?

X.G. *Yes. Is she . . . she's still enclosed in it.*

M.D. In . . .

X.G. *In . . . in her passivity.*

M.D. Yes.

X.G. *Does she bother the others?*

M.D. Yes. She bothers everybody.

X.G. *She frightens them?*

M.D. Yes. You remember at that reception she gives, everybody's ill.

X.G. *Yes. So it's . . . it acts on the others.*

M.D. Oh, yes.

X.G. *But what kind of thing is it, in relation to the other woman?*

M.D. In *La Femme du Gange*?

X.G. *Yes. The woman in black. She's passive, too, and yet she speaks;*

sometimes, very rarely, she sings.

M.D. She's mad, too, but she's mad at the end of a life that's been lived.

X.G. *Not Lol. V. Stein?*

M.D. Lol. V. Stein is mad at the end of a life that hasn't been lived.

X.G. *She couldn't live.*

M.D. Unlived. [*Loud explosion.*] That's the men setting off explosives . . .
Yes, you think Lol. V. Stein is a woman; that is, she lived in a
spectacular way, in an exem—— . . . how should I say it?—in a
distended way, basically.

X.G. *Yes, hypertrophic.*

M.D. Hypertrophic, that's what it is. The ini—— . . . initial trauma of
every woman . . .

X.G. *Maybe. In a somewhat exemplary way.*

M.D. Do you think that her movement of melting into the lovers, joining
with the lovers, to which is opposed a refusal, is the same movement
that every woman has in her to join . . . everyone and to which is
opposed a refusal to join with everyone, to join with the group,
humanity?

X.G. *Yes.*

M.D. Do you think so? . . . You could also see it that way. [*Silence.*] It's the
same harassment, that is, in the most . . . harassment isn't strong
enough . . . the same "no," that is: "No, you won't go any further."

X.G. *Yes, the rejection. Apparently, the other woman struggled.*

M.D. Yes.

X.G. *For a long time.*

M.D. But she abandoned everything; she had a lot of lovers and houses
and everything; she abandoned everything, little by little.

X.G. *That is, that for a long time she was in a . . . she was in the world
of men and . . .*

M.D. Yes. She couldn't do without men, lovers. She had a complacent
husband, a little like Anne-Marie Stretter.

X.G. *Yes, and she reminds you in certain respects of Anne-Marie Stretter.*

M.D. Yes, you could sometimes confuse them.

X.G. *Yes, sometimes I thought of her.*

M.D.   But Anne-Marie Stretter is crucified from the outside, by the intolerableness of the world, whereas—an immense region that is the world, if you will—whereas the other woman is crucified from the inside, by herself; her region is much smaller . . .

X.G.   *Yes.*

M.D.   . . . in the beginning—I'm thinking of Tatiana Karl—while she grows immense with the despair of advancing death. She is enlarged, the woman . . . the woman of . . . the woman dressed in black, the new, the previous Tatiana Karl; obviously, she takes on the dimensions of Lol. V. Stein but late in life. Dispossessed of youth and money and men. [*Silence.*] I can't believe myself that Lol. V. Stein is *the* Woman. I get lots of letters . . . [*End of the tape.*]

M.D.   Right, I can't quite believe that Lol. V. Stein illustrates a . . . the woman's situation; in the world now, any further . . . the more society . . . I can't see any further than her insertion in class society, in history, if you like. Because it's . . . maybe because I've never thought of it. There's one troubling thing, which is that I love her immensely, this Lol. V. Stein, and I can't rid myself of her. For me, she has a . . . a kind of inexhaustible grace. That's really strange, too; it contradicts what I've just said. I get lots of letters from people always telling me the same thing about Lol. V. Stein; always, always, it's "Lol. V. Stein is me." It's true that I also have men telling me, "The vice-consul is me," it's me, me. I also heard from people who said about *Hiroshima,* "It didn't happen during the war, but it's my story." But it's . . . the war is crucial, but the story, their story, drilled itself into the film and was found there just the same; people still found their own story, outside of all contexts. The most beautiful thing that's been said to me about *Lol. V. Stein* is this, from a critic, "*Lol. V. Stein* is something I wrote." [*Inaudible words.*] But the worst article I got about the book was still Jacqueline Piatier, who wrote it for *Le Monde*—that is, a woman.[67] And who took Lol. V. Stein out of her coffin? That was, after all, a man; it was Lacan.

X.G.   *Yes, but you know, you say a woman, but we know all too well that women are still usually very much men—that is, are very much*

117

alienated. Again, that's why I believe it's important for them to find
themselves among each other, because otherwise, they're such men!

M.D. Oh, it's hateful, it's really hateful. They're bosses in an office, they're captains, they're like madams in bordellos; as soon as she has authority over other women, a woman bullies them, the foremen in factories; women become madams in bordellos.

X.G. *But they take on men's roles so well; that's what's awful.*

M.D. That's it; it's demoralizing, completely demoralizing.

X.G. *That's what's really dangerous, this so-called equality—there's*
nothing worse than equality—which they're asking for now be-
tween men and women; what does it mean? It means that women
become what men are. No thanks—no thanks as far as I'm
concerned, anyway. You hear this everywhere, people who say,
"Woman has to get a better place on the social ladder; she too must
become a business executive." It's horrible. That's what's so dan-
gerous in what's happening these days, what they call an "eman-
cipation" for woman.

M.D. Yes. Because executives are men. So then, to become a good executive, women copy them.

X.G. *Exactly. And afterward, they're told, "Well, what do you want? You*
have the same thing as men." Whereas more than anything, women
must not want the same thing as men.

M.D. But you saw that bunch of ninnies in Brest . . . I think it was in Brest?

X.G. *I don't know.*

M.D. These high school girls made a declaration, "We are women, eternally; we shall marry; we shall have children." They're all fiancées of marine officers or men from Saint-Cyr.[68] [*Laughter.*] *Match* did a number on that, of course. No, but that is a common kind of stupidity; what can you do against a stupidity, learned stupidity? They're copiers. Above all, above all, woman has to be more ashamed of herself.

X.G. *Yes, but everything's set up so that she'll be ashamed of being a*
woman.

M.D. I knew a guy who was a gangster, and one day I asked him, "What do you do with your women?" He answered, "Well, they wait for us; we're very, very hard on them." So I asked, "But where?" He said, "Well, in cafes, while we play poker, they wait for us." I say, "But they must be dropping from exhaustion on those nights sometimes; you've been known to play the whole night in cafes." He says, "Yeah, they have to wait; otherwise they get hit." All right, he thought this was terrific, but finally, what's the difference? Haven't you seen society receptions where the women don't say a word for three hours at a stretch?

X.G. *It's the same thing.*

M.D. They wait. They're in disguise; they've had their hair done, they've been to the hairdresser; they've got beautiful flowered dresses.

X.G. *Yes, they're what you call feminine women! They think that's what femininity is; they're made to believe, they do believe that they're very womanly, but what are they? They're completely man-made.*

M.D. But they don't dare speak.

X.G. *But they've been told, "It's not a woman's place to speak . . . don't get involved in politics." They're told, for example, "This is men's business, men's affairs." They wait; their husbands leave for war, they wait; the men leave for the office, they wait.*

M.D. At the same time, it might be good to recall what Michelet said about witches.

X.G. *Oh, yes, tell me.*

M.D. Oh, it's great, it's in his book *La Sorcière*. By the way, I wanted to tell you earlier that he was the one . . . do you remember his book on women when he talks about menstruation, but for him it was a . . . a source of eroticism? Yes, he said that in the high Middle Ages, women were alone on their farms, in the forest, while the lord was away at war—whenever I can, I tell this story; I think it's sublime—and so they were extremely bored, alone on their farms, and they were hungry, with the man away on the Crusades or in the lord's war, and that's how women began to talk, alone, to the foxes and squirrels, to the birds, to the trees. And when the husband came back, they continued to do so. I have to add that otherwise no one would have noticed anything; but it was the men who found them speaking alone in the forest.

X.G. *And I would add: the men must have said, "They're completely crazy; this is really woman's foolishness."*

M.D. That's right, and then they burned them. To stop it, block up the madness, block up feminine speech.

X.G. *But Joan of Arc heard voices.*

M.D. Well, yes, of course. Joan of Arc is a masculine crime. Sollers told me he wasn't interested in Joan of Arc.

X.G. *Well I'm interested in her.*

M.D. I'm fascinated by her. The emphasis has always been on the woman soldier . . . on the woman in man's clothing, since it was for that that they killed her. For example, she had a political mind equal to that of Saint-Just; it's sublime, but it's never been said, precisely because she's a woman.

X.G. *But for me, I think it's amazing that she heard voices. I don't know . . .*

M.D. I think it's incredible that Charles VII obeyed her; he did what she wanted, and the soldiers followed her to Orléans. There had to be a trial to get her killed.

X.G. *Yes, a whole state apparatus.*

M.D. A whole state apparatus, a judiciary, institutional apparatus. Otherwise, it would have been a murder—which the people wouldn't have allowed, I suspect—like that of Giordano Bruno. [*Silence.*] Well, shall we stop for today?

X.G. *Yes, let's stop.*

Fifth Interview

X.G.   *You should say what you have to say about "Indiana Song."*

M.D.   I'm not sure about the title, the title of the text, the latest one.[69] I had thought of several titles. You can tell me what you think of them. There was "Les Amants du Gange" to underscore the connection between the film *La Femme du Gange* and this text, which has the advantage of showing very clearly that that's . . . that's where it came from . . . both in form and content.

X.G.   *Definitely. There's a continuity there.*

M.D.   There was "Les Iles," . . . "Les Amants du Gange," "Les Iles," "Le Ciel de mousson" . . . I don't remember the others—they're upstairs in my room, but I don't remember. There were five or six . . . "La Route du delta." "La Route du delta," "La Route de Chandernagor." There, that's all.

X.G.   *I think that already I like "Indiana Song" better. I don't know if it's because it's the one you kept, but "Les Amants du Gange"—well, it's true that there's complete continuity between that and* La Femme du Gange *. . . what bothers me is "Les Amants" . . .*

M.D.   And maybe the vice-consul who's not in it?

X.G.   *Yes, the vice-consul who's not in it and then "les amants," we're used to thinking that that means two people, whereas here . . . there are the lovers and then there's everybody else. Do you see? It's just not about a couple.*

M.D.   She's everybody's lover; she's the prostitute of Calcutta.

X.G.   *That's it, that's it. And "Indiana Song" is . . . you see, it's done to the tune, the tune of the past. I already see it as a memory, something that was said, a song that was said.*

M.D.   Like "Blue Moon" in *La Femme du Gange*.

X.G.   *Yes.*

M.D.   And the inaccuracy doesn't bother you: Indiana is in Latin America, I think.

X.G.   *Yes, well, I don't know if it's . . .*

M.D.   It's just phonetic.

X.G.   *Yes, I see. You know, it's true that geography is one thing . . . we have to keep geography in mind, India and all that. But when you say . . . the other titles you mentioned are specifically geographical. . . "Delta" . . .*

M.D.   "Le Delta," "Chandernagor."

X.G.   *Those are places.*

M.D.   "Les Iles," that's satirical.

X.G.   *You see, it's situated in space, it situates the place. With "Indiana Song," already, the place is false, since it's not India. But also Song, you see, it's the . . .*

M.D.   A-literary, you mean, almost.

X.G.   *Yes, the word, the word as it is sung. That's the title I like best, definitely.*

M.D.   I have to say right away that the geography is not at all exact. I fabricated an India, the Indies, as we used to say . . . during colonialism. Calcutta wasn't the capital, and you can't get from Calcutta to the mouth of the Ganges in one afternoon. The island is Ceylon, it's Colombo; *The Prince of Wales* of Colombo isn't there at all. As for Nepal, the French ambassador couldn't go there to hunt in a day either. And Lahore is very far away; Lahore is in Pakistan. There's nothing but ricefields there, really; they're in the delta. They're enormous; nothing's there but rice.

X.G.   *All right, then, this geography is wrong from one standpoint . . .*

M.D.   From an academic standpoint, it's wrong.

X.G.   *Yes, academic, yes, that's right. Whereas it's correct in your mind.*

It's an entirely appropriate geography for you.

M.D. It's absolutely inevitable.

X.G. *Inevitable . . .*

M.D. I can see everything, the walls of Calcutta, concentric walls, you see, which the Ganges runs right through, they're kinds of enormous sectors of water with trees along the banks, fig and tamarind trees.

X.G. *But you really get the feeling that it's unalterable. You can't change anything, not the smallest detail, you see. I mean that even if it's in your head, you get the impression that each thing is in its place, it's there, and that it couldn't be put anywhere else; that there's . . . there's an internal logic—just as much for the characters, by the way, in what they do. They could never do anything else than what they're doing, not a finger . . . could move . . . differently . . . that's what's really impressive.*

M.D. You're saying that you enter into the logic? Into my logic?

X.G. *Yes, completely; it can't be, it couldn't be changed by a hair.*

M.D. And yet you had read *Le Vice-consul* beforehand.

X.G. *Yes, of course. But inside the book, you see, it's the same; inside* Le Vice-consul *nothing can be changed. Inside "Indiana Song" nothing can be changed.*

M.D. Right.

X.G. *There are very few gestures, basically, very few spoken words, very few . . . objects that are noted, but the ones that* are *there are there inevitably. So, I don't know, I think back to that woman who said to you about* La Femme du Gange, *"How well you calculated everything!" and all that, when you don't calculate anything.*

M.D. No, nothing at all.

X.G. *But I understand why she says that, you see; it's because that's the impression you get—not that it's calculated, but that nothing's been left to chance.*

M.D. There's a kind of chemistry . . .

X.G. *Which is very precise.*

M.D. Oh, yes, but that's inside my head.

x.g.   *Right.*

m.d.   But usually it's for places. You see, I could almost factor them, place A, place B, place C, place D; and there's a crying-out at place C, cries that reach A; place D doesn't hear any cries, do you see? The English cemetery where she's buried—I don't know whether there's a bend in the Ganges there, but I see it.

x.g.   *Yes.*

m.d.   I wanted to introduce the notion of water there, a marsh; I felt it, but I couldn't do it. There's something called the leftovers of the Loire, dried-up tributaries. I don't know if there are any in the Ganges. That's how I see them.

x.g.   *Yes, you see them like that. But that's really impressive, this unfaltering vision imposed on the reader.*

m.d.   I see everything except the faces.

x.g.   *Except the faces?*

m.d.   I don't see the face of Anne-Marie Stretter. I hear her voice; I see her body, her walk especially, her walk through the gardens— she's wearing shorts—when she goes to play tennis, you see. I see the . . . I see the color of her hair, it's red, and she has blond eyelashes. I see that too. Her eyes are somewhat sunken; they're very light-colored eyes, you know, very light eyes in the sunlight, if you see what I mean, but her features and her expression I don't see.

x.g.   *That's odd. But is it because from the beginning she contains her death?*

m.d.   Maybe it's that I never see faces. Maybe it's that . . . the face comes last.

x.g.   *Oh, yes. For the vice-consul you say it's like a face that's grafted onto a body.*

m.d.   Yes, the vice-consul is made out of bits and pieces. It's as if he has a borrowed voice, a grafted-on face, yes, a walk that's not his—a bit like a Picasso, you know.

x.g.   *It's almost as if nothing is his.*

m.d.   No, nothing is his.

X.G.   . . . *of himself. He doesn't possess any of himself.*

M.D.   No, but that can be explained, I think. He's not the vice-consul, you can't be the vice-consul—or he never would have lived. So he's made of bits and pieces, out of all their despair, you see, from the voice of . . . from an impossible, inaudible voice . . . the voice of a madman, do you see?

X.G.   *Yes.*

M.D.   He's got the voice of a madman.

X.G.   *Yes, but even his act, the only act, really, that he performed, that is, to shoot at the lepers and the dogs—not even his act belongs to him.*

M.D.   No, it's a dictated act. But from very far away, though. There's that sentence from Breton.

X.G.   *To shoot at random into the crowd?*

M.D.   Yes, when you're twenty years old.

X.G.   *Yes, to get out the revolvers and shoot at random into the crowd.*

M.D.   Yes.

X.G.   *It's strange, because it somehow makes more sense to me in Breton. It seems nonsensical, it seems irrational, and yet in Breton you can still say what the reason is. Something like: one has to revolt against society; one has to . . . whatever; you see things like that. Yes, we have to revolt against society. Whereas it seems to me that with the vice-consul . . .*

M.D.   . . . the revolt is already there . . . in childhood; it's not something reasoned.

X.G.   *Right, there isn't even the desire to revolt.*

M.D.   But you can't like him!

X.G.   *The vice-consul?*

M.D.   You'd chase him away if he were near you; he's unbearable.

X.G.   *He'd be terrifying.*

M.D.   He's unbearable. And you can tell that he's dead. That is, he's not dead; he's life itself, since he can't stand anything, since life is expressed as refusal in my books, right? The more you refuse, the more you're opposed, the more you live.

X.G.   *Yes.*

M.D.   People are asses, but we know that. It's such tremendous stupidity to see refusal as death; it's life.

X.G.   *Yes, and* him, *he's refusal incarnate. He's complete refusal.*

M.D.   Yes.

X.G.   *To the point that he refuses—that's what's so admirable, too—to the point that he refuses to justify his act.*

M.D.   That's right.

X.G.   *Because that's . . . when you make some kind of refusal, as soon as you justify it, it's done for.*

M.D.   But I don't think he even knows.

X.G.   *No.*

M.D.   He gets up. He sees from his balcony in the dawn—the Indian dawn . . . the dawn of the monsoon, which is horrible, it's gray, heavy, the heat relentless at five o'clock in the morning—he sees the lepers huddled together and . . . and I think there's a White man he knows there . . . he shoots into the pain, he makes it explode. But he's shooting just as much at God as at society.

X.G.   *And at himself.*

M.D.   And at himself.

X.G.   *Yes, yes. When I say that he refuses to justify his act, it's not that he's saying, "I won't justify it"; it's that he can't. It's a complete refusal, it's internal, in him.*

M.D.   He can't.

X.G.   *And in* Le Vice-consul, *but also in "Indiana Song," that's really what bothers people, and they keep coming back to his act, trying to justify it, trying to prove something. The society talk in the embassy, the women's just as much as the men's, is about that: "But he really did it, but how did it happen? But . . ."*

M.D.   They always limit themselves to the literal facts. He killed. "The poor lepers," they say. Do you understand?

X.G.   *Yes.*

M.D.   It's not enough to die from leprosy; he kills them. But it's leprosy that's killing them.

126

x.g.   *Yes, but it seems to me that they're trying to give a meaning to his act.*

m.d.   Oh, of course.

x.g.   *That's what the catastrophe is, whereas it's not about . . .*

m.d.   . . . bringing him back to psychology; but they can't do it.

x.g.   *No, they can't.*

m.d.   They can't manage it at all. It's the path of fraternity, you notice, in one sense . . . If they could do it, maybe the vice-consul could be admitted . . .

x.g.   *Yes, but do you think that's desirable?*

m.d.   What he did is beyond reclamation.

x.g.   *Yes, but they try to salvage it.*

m.d.   Yes, they do.

x.g.   *They do it saying, for example, "How unfortunate!" or by saying . . . saying . . . by making psychological, moral judgments. Whereas in fact it has nothing to do with that, really, and there's only Anne-Marie Stretter who . . . who accepts that act completely without . . . without trying [to impose] anything at all.*

m.d.   Yes, that's to say there's an equivalence. It's more than an identification; there's an equivalence between Anne-Marie Stretter's pain and the French vice-consul's anger. It flows in her, you see, like a river that's traveled through her; it's as if she's tunneled by this river of pain, if you like, whereas he, by contrast . . . is like an engine of . . . well, of death; he's full of fire, and explosives, finally . . . all that has to get out, burst; it has to get expressed on the outside, be public, loud, whereas the entry . . . Anne-Marie Stretter's entry within India is . . . is carnal. It's internal.

x.g.   *Yes, but the gesture* she *makes, giving water to the lepers, giving them food . . .*

m.d.   I couldn't care less about that, in the . . .

x.g.   *Yes, that's what it is; it's the day of good deeds.*

m.d.   . . . in the reception. It's the classic, cultural good deed. But *she* knows very well what it's about. She just leaves the embassy gates open so that the beggars can enter, but I do not for a second praise the act.

X.G.   *That's right, no, because in the extreme, like that, it could seem to be in opposition to the vice-consul's act, while I think that in the last analysis it's done with the same despair.*

M.D.   Absolutely. I hope that it never for a second looks like a . . .

X.G.   *Like a solution? [Laughter.] Charity! . . .*

M.D.   I hope not.

X.G.   *Really, that would be impossible. All the more so since it's the society women who, during the reception, talk about it; they say, "What an irreproachable woman!"*

M.D.   Yes, but they also know that she's going . . . that she sleeps with everyone.

X.G.   *Yes, but from the standpoint of what's "good"—that is, what they call the good—that she gives food to the beggars. So if it's the women themselves who say so . . .*

M.D.   It's not said that she's good, or charitable. In the book, though, it was said.

X.G.   *But, the women say . . . they still say "good," in "Indiana Song."*

M.D.   They say "irreproachable."

X.G.   *"Irreproachable: she gives water to the . . ."*

M.D.   Yes, but irreproachable in general. There's someone who says, "Irreproachable? Now, come on." And someone else adds, "Nothing shows, that's what we mean here by irreproachable."

X.G.   *That's right; they meant that there was no scandal as there had been for the vice-consul. You can do what you want so long as it doesn't show. That's the principle . . .*

M.D.   That's right. While with the vice-consul there's the outcry, the scandal . . .

X.G.   *Yes, that's what's intolerable.*

M.D.   All the time.

X.G.   *All those people can endure Anne-Marie Stretter's being completely ripped apart, completely dead, as long as it doesn't show, as long as she has a smile so that they can fool themselves.*

M.D. But they don't . . . know, they sense it . . .

X.G. *They don't want to know.*

M.D. . . . that she is pain. She'll never say it; it's never avowed, since when she cries and tears come out, she doesn't feel them; she always says, "It's the light that hurts my eyes, the light of the monsoon." It's not by chance that this is India. It's the world center of absurdity, the main fire of absurdity, this insane, illogical conglomeration of hunger and famine.

X.G. *That is to say, there's absurdity in our world, too, but you see it less. It's more obvious in India.*

M.D. That's right, in India it's visible immediately. This text is religious at heart, isn't it?

X.G. *How do you mean, religious?*

M.D. I mean . . . because it refuses the real, refuses it as far as it does, cries out against the real of India—I'm not calling this "reality"; it's an . . . overused word—by, yes, by dint of crying out against it; it's as if there were someone responsible for this state of affairs.

X.G. *It's funny that you think that. The word "religious" shocks me. Would the one responsible be God?*[70]

M.D. Yes, it's not true, it's not . . . it's an order of things, yes, the one responsible is humanity who let this happen . . . but it let it happen in the same way that we sleep, as we live . . . without knowing what's happening.

X.G. *Yes, but it's all the relations . . . all the human relations on which society is based that are in question.*

M.D. Yes. The watertight relationship between the world of White India and this other one is denounced all through the book.

X.G. *But why do you say religious, then? . . . where I myself would almost say that it's political.*

M.D. I think it has a meaning . . . Well, maybe it's the same thing. I've been told—I don't know whether I told you—I've been told that I'm religious . . . that I've got the religious sense of Communism.

x.g.   *No. You didn't tell me. It shocks me a little. [Silence.] Or else I'd have to understand religion to mean that there's something that is beyond us.*

m.d.   Again, it's the transgression, from oneself to the other.

x.g.   *But it's something that we are, too.*

m.d.   But that should be a meaning of man and not a concept. There's no slippage in that White humanity in India toward . . . hunger, toward pain, leprosy. There's a continual safeguard for the White.

x.g.   *Except, it's just that . . . this safeguard is broken . . .*

m.d.   It's broken; contact is made through . . . through pain, through Anne-Marie Stretter's tears, made tangibly, organically, and through the vice-consul's gunshots.

x.g.   *Yes.*

m.d.   Otherwise, it's watertight, between this and the others.

x.g.   *But exactly; this transgression, you say, is organic, is tangible.*

m.d.   Yes.

x.g.   *Whereas "religious," it seems, goes back to . . . to a world . . .*

m.d.   By "religious" I think of that silent surge that's stronger than oneself and unjustifiable.

x.g.   *Yes, yes, that's right, something in us that's beyond us, is stronger than we are . . . it's in us.*

m.d.   . . . and that silences . . . logical reason.

x.g.   *Yes, and psychological commentaries. Yes, yes, that's something I really understand, but why use the word "religion"? That, you understand, is what . . .*

m.d.   It was used in connection with *Jaune le soleil.*

x.g.   *. . . whereas . . . what do you expect, you can't . . . it's borrowed from . . . all right, it means everything that . . . at the same time, everything you abhor, doesn't it?*

m.d.   Oh, yes, of course. Of course.

x.g.   *You can't separate it from the context . . .*

m.d.   No, but it's . . . religious isn't religion. "Christian without God"— that's in the book, you see, in connection with her.

x.g. *Yes.*

m.d. And you accepted that?

x.g. *Yes.*

m.d. You cannot, cannot get caught up on words.

x.g. *Yes, that's what I'm doing. But . . . but I'm afraid that it's kind of dangerous still, to use that word. Even if I really understand the meaning you give it, you see, since in society it has an unshakable meaning.*

m.d. It's being shaken up, though, more and more.

x.g. *Don't you think, in any event, that it goes back to all that . . . you know, to metaphysics, that whole universe . . .*

m.d. In *La Femme du Gange*, she says, "What's wrong with you? You don't eat anymore, you don't sleep anymore," and she says, "It's anger." They ask her, "At what?" and she answers, "At God, God in general."

x.g. *Yes, I remember that. Yes, that really struck me, and there I understand it really well, you see.*

m.d. But read it as something else; you have to understand it as something else.

x.g. *But in this case, I really understand it.*

m.d. Yes.

x.g. *Even Lol. V. Stein, I think, she says . . . something against God.*

m.d. Oh? I don't remember.

x.g. *No, wait. There's a . . . moment during her sickness . . . well, what's called her sickness, how does it go? "moving around in the belly of God" . . . it's something like that. Why can't I remember that phrase?*

m.d. Oh, you're right, that rings a bell.

x.g. *Just at the end of the chapter, of the whole chapter about her sickness, afterward you see her . . . you see her differently, you see her married—wait, there's all her anger, all her refusal, all her . . . so that she doesn't see anything anymore, doesn't hear anything anymore. And then there's a phrase, ". . . moving around in the belly* of God." I don't know, something like that.[71] And I found that really extraordinary. There I understood it very well and accepted it very easily.

M.D. But what does the vice-consul's anger stand out against and the . . . Anne-Marie Stretter's latent, constant suffering? [*Silence.*] They stand out against the unlivable.

X.G. *Yes.*

M.D. And against love.

X.G. *Yes, but that's not religious.*

M.D. Love isn't?

X.G. *No.*

M.D. It's not Marxist. Maybe it's anti-Marxism that I'm expressing with this. The text I've just done is a political text, do you agree?

X.G. *Yes, absolutely.*

M.D. Completely, yes. But a Marxist-Leninist . . . of average intelligence wouldn't understand it. The truth must be told. When Marxism-Leninism hits someone over the head . . . someone average, of average capacity—it's sad, but you have to say it—it sometimes replaces the absent intelligence.

X.G. *It's disastrous.*

M.D. It's disastrous, because feeling used to fill in in the absence of intelligence, in the absence of arguments, in the absence of quibbling; feeling would fill in for intelligence, because there are feelings of genius. Only in the . . . in the . . . how do I say this? in Marxist-Leninist practice, feeling ceases to function.

X.G. *In any case, it's put to the service of something else, it's . . .*

M.D. It's silenced. The individual has silenced it. He uses his . . . he's thrilled because his Marxism-Leninism, so he believes, opens the doors of his mind.

X.G. *It takes the cake. It's the answer to everything.*

M.D. Right. A man who was unarmed, who was in a state of naiveté, gets arms.

X.G. *Yes, he finds ready-made weapons.*

M.D. Yes. I was driven out of the party by people like that.

X.G. *Yes. I can well understand what you're saying.*

M.D. You can even go further than that: you can also say that theoretical practice obliterates the rest.

X.G. *Wait. I don't agree.*

M.D. . . . very often.

X.G. *But now look, what I wanted to say for Marxism . . .*

M.D. Yes.

X.G. *When you say, that . . . that the book is anti-Marxist . . .*

M.D. . . . formally.

X.G. *I think that . . .*

M.D. I mean formally. What's given in India, in "Indiana Song" what's given to see—the givens given to see, you could say—aren't Marxist givens.

X.G. *I'll tell you what I think. I think that what strict Marxism needs is to . . .*

M.D. . . . forget Marxism. [*Laughter.*]

X.G. *Yes, among other things. But I mean the articulation with desire— let's say that this knowledge can be articulated—all right, of exploitation . . . with . . .*

M.D. It's fruitless.

X.G. *. . . with desire.*

M.D. It's fruitless, an experience . . .

X.G. *Yes. Whereas precisely in "Indiana Song," it is articulated, and completely, completely interwoven—desire, love, you see, it's . . .*

M.D. Well, desire is a movement toward the other. Which is an apprehension . . . a prehension of the other and the pain lived by Anne-Marie Stretter, equally.

X.G. *Yes, yes, but it's completely fused, that's the point, with . . .*

M.D. It's that the two movements are movements toward, movements that put one outside oneself, place you outside yourself.

X.G. *Yes, yes. And at the same time, it's completely caught up with, I don't know, denunciation, the refusal of exploitation, of misery.*

M.D. It *is* refusal.

X.G. *It's the same thing. It's completely fused together.*

M.D.   But a Marxist would say, "Watch out, there can't be any sentiment."

X.G.   *But it's not sentiment.*

M.D.   Yes, well, precisely; he'd still confuse it.

X.G.   *Well, yes, but there's no sentiment in your book. It's not sentiment. It's something that . . . that burns, that floors you, that . . . that has physical effects, cries and tears; it's not sentiment. Don't you agree?*

M.D.   Yes, I'm completely with you.

X.G.   *That's why it's not anti-Marxist. It's just that it offers the whole dimension that Marxism is missing, not that it goes against it.*

M.D.   Yes, that is, behind it you can sense a political experience that lasted for twenty years and ended in a fiasco but is there nonetheless.

X.G.   *Yes, the experience isn't denied; it's not denied. You sense it.*

M.D.   That is to say that not only do I despair of society but I despair of revolution. Even so, I still denounce society by means of arms . . . revolutionary arms. But all that is forgotten when I write.

X.G.   *Yes.*

M.D.   It's there but forgotten, just like the culture that has to be forgotten.

X.G.   *Yes, that is, it's not . . . you don't want to say something; it is said, you don't mean . . . when you write, you don't mean: "It's shameful what's happening in India."*

M.D.   Ah, l don't want to be declarative.

X.G.   *That's right.*

M.D.   That's all over, it's . . . because once I was, a little bit, in *Le Barrage*.

X.G.   *In your early books.*

M.D.   But even here, the old woman who discourses invents a personal dialectic . . . It happens that this dialectic, given the fact that she's oppressed and in a colonized country, is akin to a revolutionary dialectic. But it's her own invention.
       [*End of the tape.*]

M.D.   There's always a little dead time when we change sides.

X.G.   *Yes, that's true; it's a pain. Because we forget, like I forgot the other time. [Silence.]*

M.D.   You see, what's just happened in South Africa, that drought that caused I don't know how many deaths, 80 percent of the animals died, and trees . . . that was happening at the same time as you and your life, as me and my life, as the lives of . . . all our contemporaries, and it's completely obliterated. It's unbearable; it's literally unbearable, and luckily, it's obliterated from everyday life, but it's still there.

X.G. *Yes, but, you don't think that . . .*

M.D. You can't deny it.

X.G. *. . . what also stands out, for example, in "Indiana Song" . . .*

M.D. Young people told me, "We weren't part of the war; we don't know what it means; we weren't part of the concentration camps, the extermination of the Jews . . . *We don't know what that is.* After *Hiroshima,* I had a discussion with them here at N——. I said, "That's not true, *you do know* something."

X.G. *Yes.*

M.D. Even if it's pushed back. *One knows.* It's something that's known. People always say, "We don't know about it." That's indifference. But somewhere, it is known.

X.G. *Yes.*

M.D. Otherwise, the Whites at the reception, the White women at the reception wouldn't be as intrigued by Anne-Marie Stretter as they are. They say, "That heartrending smile, what does it hide? What's she doing?" They ask themselves questions.

X.G. *Yes.*

M.D. But it's through the mediation of this woman. They don't see India directly. They see it through these bridges, these relays, which are the vice-consul, that balcony at Lahore, and here, the woman's tears. That's what it's for, these writings, the written. It's this relaying, maybe, this bridge thrown across.

X.G. *. . . which means that we can no longer ignore what we know inside us, that it's there somewhere.*

M.D. Yes, exactly. It's like a well: you go to look for water inside, and this water . . . people recognize this water, they drink it . . . somewhere inside them.[72] [*Silence.*] What is there to say about this form? That's the . . . you know that was the request Peter Hall made, from the National Theater.

X.G. *Yes. Why do you say that?*

M.D. Because I have to say it.

X.G. *Yes, but it seems so strange now.*

M.D. It was a request.

X.G. *Yes. But you would have written it anyway. Exactly what difference did it make that it was requested?*

M.D. It means that I did it.

X.G. *You think that you would have been able to keep it inside you?*

M.D. I could say: it means I got rid of it. It's painful.

X.G. *This was the thing that pushes from the outside so that it'll get out.*

M.D. Yes. I've never been asked to do anything in France.

X.G. *No.*

M.D. I've been asked to do things in Germany.

X.G. *All right. You could say, really, that the state of the theater in France—well, you have to see it for what it is. And for it to be England that thought of that, do you see . . . since there's something not quite right in France.*

M.D. It's more *my* situation in France.

X.G. *Oh now, listen . . .*

M.D. It's funny. Well, we've already talked about that; it's not very interesting. Here, what do I do? I pay my taxes . . . It's true I have friends here. I have friends in France. So, they get my taxes. But the money, what I'm earning now . . . what I live on, is German, American, and English.

X.G. *But also there's—I'd really like for you to talk about this, what you were saying the other day about this refusal, because it doesn't interest you either, the . . . how do I say this? the social benefits that writers generally get from their writing: doing lectures, being well-known, getting invited . . .*

M.D. There are two things here. First, it bothers me to leave home; it bothers me to live with young people for three weeks at a time. Young people are very nice, but there's nothing more uniform.

x.g. *It's true.*

m.d. It's only at twenty-seven or twenty-eight that a person begins to be differentiated. It gets on my nerves to spend the whole day with students asking me questions, never to be alone, solitary. And then, I really have nothing at all to say to them. If I spend three weeks talking about myself like that, I'll go crazy. Oh, I've refused to go anywhere, anywhere. I have no theory of the novel. Just the idea makes me laugh.

x.g. *But that's what you were saying the other day, that since you don't accept these things, you don't even get the . . . what is it? the compensation, the . . . that a lot of writers have . . .*

m.d. Money?

x.g. *Um, yes, or glory* [laughter], *or . . .*

m.d. Yes, but it's so . . . it's such a racket!

x.g. *Yes, but it must be easier for them to get by.*

m.d. After *Hiroshima,* I had that glory . . . that social glory. But you know, it's hell. People invite you to dinner to show you off like an animal they bought and especially tamed. It went on for three or four months, and then after that I skipped out. I caught on.

x.g. *But you were saying that men, in general . . .*

m.d. Men live a lot off that, off that kind of commodity, the glory, being famous. Look, it's useful, sometimes.

x.g. *Yes, it is. It must be easier for them to get by, then, if they have that. If they like it, if they have the benefit of social pleasure, a bonus . . .*

m.d. Then, austerity . . . What do you expect a Druon, an ass like him, to do with austerity . . . I mean . . . since his material, the material he works on, is already corrupted, a material that trips along in the social world, in what's bad. [*Silence.*] Maybe we could talk about "Indiana Song" some more.

x.g. *Sure.*

m.d. You see, *Lol. V. Stein,* for example, belongs more to you others now.

x.g. *It's more . . .*

m.d. It belongs more to all of you than to me. The book was so much seized upon by people that I've been dispossessed of it. As for *Moderato,* it's completely finished.

X.G. *And it's happening now with* Lol. V. Stein?

M.D. Yes, it's in the process. With *Le Vice-consul,* that was still . . . what is it called? those hidden things?

X.G. *Latent?*

M.D. It's a space for forbidden things. Everyone has this space in their lives. A place where you put things, in a mess, you call that a forbidden place. All right, that's a remark . . . a little side comment.

X.G. *No, it's not an aside. But, what effect does that have on you, knowing that people took hold of it . . .*

M.D. It's normal. I think it's normal. But Lol. V. Stein circulates now. She's an adult.

X.G. *She's living.*

M.D. Yes.

X.G. *Inside the . . . around. But that . . .*

M.D. Well, why did I add those voices? All right, there's a story given— and even that's mysterious—a story that's given, which was the vice-consul's story. It took place in a book; it encompassed certain characters, who were named, who were seen, who did things. Now then, here I am taking up that story again, and I have it told by voices which are themselves prey to their own stories; that is, if you like, at first they're distracted by the story of the vice-consul and Anne-Marie Stretter, but little by little they possess it to the point of becoming inflamed by it, I mean completely. Why this supplementary stage? And why does this supplementary stage give so much power—I have to acknowledge that, because I've just reread the . . . the text—to that story which really, it could be argued, was enough in itself?

X.G. *I don't know why, but it's true that it provides an incredible force . . . I don't know; I tell myself: maybe . . . if things are right in front of you—that is, for example, on a stage—you have people and their voices come out of their mouths; you see it, and perhaps you can still master it in a way, through the gaze, for example. If it*

> *comes from the outside, if what happens, what . . . what gets*
> *inflamed, is from the outside, you don't see it; it falls on top of you*
> *in a way . . . that's even more implacable, even more inevitable.*

M.D. Yes, you mean that a couple would make love on stage . . . and it
would be less violent . . .

X.G. *You could control that, in seeing it.*

M.D. . . . than if one told you, someone you couldn't see: "They're making
love now, right there, over on that side."

X.G. *Right. But you can't . . . you can't get a grip on it. You see, it*
happens to us completely from outside, as it happens to you in a
way from the outside, as you say. Well, not outside, but it happens
to you in a way that's relentless.

M.D. To me?

X.G. *Yes.*

M.D. Yes.

X.G. *But now, when you read it, it's . . . that's how it happens . . . you*
see, it doesn't happen right in front of you.

M.D. It doesn't happen right in front of you, that's the right phrase
exactly.

X.G. *And what can you do about it? That's how you're completely taken*
in by it. You can't do anything about it.

M.D. Yes, but given the fact that it doesn't happen out front, it could
possibly not exist. When they say, "In the background, there are
steamships from the South Pacific Lines, and to the side there's a
boating harbor, and further back there are palm trees, palm groves."
And there's nothing there.

X.G. *So, it exists even more than if you saw it, all the stronger.*

M.D. It exists where? At the theater or in the reading?

X.G. *In the reading. It exists more strongly than if it were described as*
something you had before your eyes. I'm sure about that.

M.D. But how did I find out how to do that? I wonder if it isn't the
cinema.

X.G. *Right, already in* La Femme du Gange . . .

M.D. That's where I found it, that's where I found it.

x.g.   *Yes, but it's even stronger—don't you think?—in "Indiana Song."*

m.d.   Yes. In normal theater procedure—let's take the theater as the
       rule—you've got the auditorium and you've got the stage, where
       things happen. Between the auditorium and the stage there's
       constant, direct communication.

x.g.   *Yes.*

m.d.   Here, you have the auditorium, you have the stage, and you have
       another space. It's in this other space that the things are . . . lived,
       and the stage is only an echo chamber. On stage, there's . . . for
       example, the reception—it's far away . . . fragments from the recep-
       tion come through, little pieces; people pass by at an angle and then
       disappear . . . So how does it happen that the frustration (you have
       to say this) the frustration from such a total theatrical action—since
       there are vestiges of movements, snatches of dancing, not a single
       straightforward conversation—that fascination gets grafted onto this
       frustration so . . . violently? I just can't understand it.

x.g.   *I don't really know.*

m.d.   Certainly, there's a connection with something that's escaping us
       now.

x.g.   *Yes, maybe as long as there is, as you say, the stage on one side and
       the audience in front, the audience can think that it's not about
       them anyway, since it's in front, on stage.*

m.d.   Yes, that's quite right.

x.g.   *If it doesn't come from on stage, where does it come from? It can
       come from them.*

m.d.   It's in them.

x.g.   *In them.*

m.d.   But which is the darkroom for them? Is it the stage where not a
       word is said, or that space where everything happens invisibly? Is it
       the stage that is seen, where nothing happens, or that other space
       we spoke about where everything happens? The darkroom is what I
       call the reading room.

x.g.   *It's that other space . . .*

M.D.   It's that other space. The stage being only an antechamber, clear consciousness.

X.G.   *Yes, yes, that's how it seems to me. But I tell you, the fright it gave me, the . . . the way it terrorized me, that I can't escape. Whereas maybe it's precisely not something . . . even if you're not on stage, you're not in front of a reading either, since it comes over the side.*

M.D.   That's good what you just said, "in front of a reading."

X.G.   *That's also why I like to have this particularity, this difficulty in reading—since you have to read from one side to another, you can't read . . . it's not up in front of you even for reading.*

M.D.   Not even typographically, you mean.

X.G.   *Yes, yes, whether it's written on the left, what happens—or what doesn't happen, for that matter . . .*

M.D.   Don't you think there's something like this: that the thing seen and heard, that you receive full in the face of a stage, in a straight line—in front of it, as you say—that this is a violence, an oppression.

X.G.   *For the viewer?*

M.D.   Yes.

X.G.   *Yes, that is, for him it's passivity.*

M.D.   . . . that we've gotten to such a point, now, in desiring freedom, that it . . . it struggles inside us; we can't stand that anymore, maybe.

X.G.   *I don't know.*

M.D.   Didn't you feel a relief in reading "Indiana Song," from that standpoint, that it comes from a freer field, farther away, and that it doesn't trip you up as soon as you go back into the reading? Didn't you have that?

X.G.   *What I didn't experience was that passivity that's usually asked of the reader; that is, he's told, "This is the way it is . . ."*

M.D.   Yes.

X.G.   *And here . . . and here, it's almost . . . what I think might seem idiotic, but it's almost as if it were I who . . . who was doing it at the same time I was reading it, you see.*

M.D.   Yes, that's right, that's right, you're the one who does it . . . yes . . .

x.g. *But that is not to say . . . I couldn't have changed a thing, you see; that was exactly it. But at the same time, I was the one who was writing it, who . . . I was the one who was saying it.*

m.d. When I say, "She passes through; she comes back to the French residence over the beaches and the men come back through the palm groves," those are your palm groves, your beaches. Right?

x.g. *Oh, yes.*

m.d. But in the theater, you are shown neither the palms nor the . . . neither the palm groves nor the beaches, you understand—but Racine would describe them. Anyone and everyone describes what beaches are like: the light, the . . . whatever, whereas a word would be enough.

x.g. *Yes. A word, the way it's said, the way it's placed in relation to another one.*

m.d. Yes.

x.g. *It's very, very precise, also, the way the words are placed, you know. You can't place them otherwise.*

m.d. But certainly there's . . . a weariness in . . . in this work I've just done; it expresses a weariness with something, with theatrical regimentation.

x.g. *Traditional, you mean?*

m.d. Yes.

x.g. *Yes. There's something there that . . .*

m.d. The walls of the stage had to be smashed.

x.g. *Yes . . . which completely exploded. The relation that the actor and the creator have to the viewer is completely changed.*

m.d. And you can sense this even in reading?

x.g. *Oh, yes. It's the same, the relation to the reading is completely changed. You don't read it like a . . . like, I don't know, what you usually read, like a novel.*

m.d. Notice that this is a beginning; I'm sure we ought to find other paths of revival, other new paths—it's not even revival—new ones.

x.g. *Yes, but this is one, it's new, revolutionary—you can say revolutionary. Everything's changed.*

M.D. You wanted to talk about something when I started on this digression.

X.G. *I don't remember. You think so?*

M.D. Wasn't it about Lol. V. Stein?

X.G. *Oh, right. But look, I'm the one who's going to digress now. It's that I was thinking about what you had said, after* Détruire, *because you said you are fundamentally dispossessed of Lol. V. Stein, that the public possesses her as much as you do, at least as much. What you had told about, what had happened after* Détruire, *because it was the same thing, you see. Do you remember what I mean?*

M.D. The anecdote I told?

X.G. *Yes, but that's not . . . it's more than an anecdote. Don't you want to tell it?*

M.D. Oh . . . but people will see it as bragging.

X.G. *Well, they'd be stupid. It's the reason people can take hold of Lol. V. Stein or of someone in* Détruire, *because it doesn't belong to you any more than to others.*

M.D. It's just that I was . . . , yes . . . I was having lunch with some friends and they were talking about *Détruire,* and this wasn't very long ago; it's . . . it was three months ago.

X.G. *Yes?*

M.D. One of my friends said, "You know I got into the film right away, but I didn't get into the book immediately." And without skipping a beat, I said, "Hey, that's strange, because I got into the book right away." Then they all looked at me. But that only lasted a few seconds; then they all laughed. In short, I had forgotten that I'd written it, it's . . . But they hadn't forgotten.

X.G. *Well, of course not, but still, it seems that to that extent you're not like other writers, like most writers, someone who possesses—you know, like the propertied: what they write, you see, they hook onto; it's their personal possession. With you, other people can possess it too, readers can. It's the same thing that you said happened with Lol. V. Stein, isn't it?*

M.D. It becomes theirs, you mean?

143

X.G. *Yes.*

M.D. Yes. But Kévork Kuttukdjian says, "*I'm* the one who wrote *Lol. V. Stein.*" I love it that someone can say that.

X.G. *Do you realize . . . And that has to do with you, that has to do with the way you write. If people think that it's bragging to say that . . . but it's completely . . . it's humility, not in the Christian sense, but in the . . . true sense: that is, not putting yourself in charge of something. Look at the vice-consul—he doesn't put himself in charge of his act.*

M.D. No. But you see, I have . . . I know someone who wanted to meet me because of *Le Vice-consul* and who is writing a book, a novel, and he asked to insert passages from *Le Vice-consul* into the novel, long passages, chapters sometimes, with no indication of their origin. I accepted, of course.

X.G. *You accepted?*

M.D. Well, of course. Gladly.

X.G. *You see, that's it . . . do you know many writers, just between us, who would do that, who would accept that?*

M.D. Oh, listen, it seems to me—I don't know—it's . . .

X.G. *It seems to you? People cling much too much to their . . .*

M.D. The book has become like a person; it belongs to the domain of the imaginary in this young man who's writing the book.

X.G. *Yes.*

M.D. You have to disconnect it from its . . . from its handicap of being part of the written, get it out of this straitjacket of the written, this straitjacket that's regarded as sacred.

X.G. *Yes . . .*

M.D. It has to circulate.

X.G. *Yes. I would say, more than what's written, it's . . . what's sacred is the author . . . the author set up as . . . the sacred author—well, the sacred idea of the author.*

M.D. It's asses who think like that.

X.G. *Well yes, but . . .*

M.D. You see, the text of *Hiroshima* has become like a song.

X.G. *Yes, it circulates, it belongs . . .*

M.D. It's been said. It really shocked me a bit because I was still
somewhat dense at the time—I'm less so now—it shocked me
because there were strippers who would recite it in the . . . in
Parisian striptease clubs: "You're killing me, you're good for me."

X.G. *That does seem weird, but . . .*

M.D. But why not?

X.G. *Well, exactly.*

M.D. Why not? The more texts circulate, whether they're political or not,
the better it is. To come back to what the theoretician of the
Nouveau Roman says—what's his name?

X.G. *Robbe-Grillet?*

M.D. No, the one who did *Pour un nouveau roman*, Ricardou, he said,
"They write a Mallarmé poem in Paris and the consequences are . . .
they're felt as far as South Africa." But I'm very confident about—I
have to say this—about what I do; no matter what criticism says or
does, I'm very confident about what I do.

X.G. *Of course you are.*

M.D. Does it show?

X.G. *Yes, but it's not at all an assurance like . . .*

M.D. I'm in an abominable state of doubt . . .

X.G. *Yes. That's right, it's not a certainty about yourself.*

M.D. . . . about the act of writing, if you will.

X.G. *It's a kind of certainty that can only be this: that this comes out of
you, and that in any event it can only be this; and it's* this *that's
right, isn't it?*

M.D. Maybe.

X.G. *No, but tell me, because if I'm putting words in your mouth now!*

M.D. It's what is written, yes, that's right.

X.G. *That's it, that's what I mean.*

M.D. That it was I who wrote it . . . that's not . . . that's much less
important.

X.G. *That's right. I don't believe at all that you're sure of yourself, but
you are of what's written. You can't deceive yourself.*

[There's been the sound of barking since the beginning of the tape; at this point, it becomes quite loud.]

M.D.   Oh, that dog out there!

X.G.   *You know that comes out really loud on the tape.*

M.D.   Okay, let's play it back to see.
[*We listen.*]

X.G.   *No, it doesn't cover the words at all. [Silence.] Well, there we go; we've got another . . . another hiatus.*

M.D.   Ask me some questions if you like. You had noted down things, you said, that you wanted to ask me.

X.G.   *Yes, but not about "Indiana Song."*

M.D.   No, but whatever.
[*Interruption.*]

X.G.   *. . . this is about what you were saying, that when you write something new, you repeat certain things from your books. You partially forget them; you "mis remember."*

M.D.   Yes, because the new thing replaces it.

X.G.   *Replaces it, yes, but that's also because you've forgotten . . .*

M.D.   Yes.

X.G.   *. . . what you wrote, to the point of forgetting that you wrote it.*

M.D.   That's right. [*Laughter.*]

X.G.   *Which is really as far as you can go.*

M.D.   Now, that really makes you believe in my good intentions, I think.

X.G.   *Oh yes, totally. Totally.*

M.D.   For example, it occurs to me . . . I remember having asked—was it you?—if there was the woman in *L'Amour.*

X.G.   *Yes, yes, it was me.*

M.D.   Well, anyway, is she there or not? I couldn't say, right away, whether she is or not. She isn't there?

X.G.   *The woman in black?*

M.D.   Yes.

X.G.   *Listen, I don't know how to answer you because the woman in black—is she also the woman in* L'Amour?

M.D.   Oh, the woman in *L'Amour* is Lol. V. Stein.

x.g.   *Yes, but is she . . .*

m.d.   But aren't there two women in *L'Amour?*

x.g.   *No, no, there's only one.*

m.d.   Well then, you see, I don't know that.

x.g.   *Is that what you're asking?*

m.d.   Yes.

x.g.   *Oh no, there's only one.*

m.d.   And I wrote it just a year ago!

x.g.   *Yes, precisely; that also makes me think of when your friends looked askance after you said that, when they said, "Something's wrong." Once you said that men had always held in front of you the bogeyman of madness.*

m.d.   It wasn't especially men, but there was a kind of language concerning me, and people don't pay enough attention to it; at the drop of a hat, they'd say, "You're really crazy," "You're even crazier than we thought," "You'd better be careful, you're really cracked," "Oh, you, you're crazy, so be quiet" . . . You know—you know, I mean, it was the plural that made me say the formal you[73]—those little things people say to children, when they harp on the same old story; it gets to you finally and creates a little . . . a little neurosis or whatever.[74] Yes, I was really afraid.

x.g.   *An anxiety. But it's like—hey, I remember when you had gone to Rome, at the airport there; you could tell that story, too, when you stayed a whole day without . . .*

m.d.   But what happened there? Nobody knows.

x.g.   *But you said that afterward they looked at you so strangely, as if . . .*

m.d.   That is, I think I really frightened them. Yes, I went to Rome and then I . . . It was to try to have *Détruire* put on by someone besides me, because all the producers I'd seen in Paris said, "Fine, we'll take the book right away but only if it's not you who films it." So I had gone to Rome to see Nello Risi. And I was supposed to meet with some producers there at the airport. I arrived at noon. I didn't see the producers. Apparently, they were there, but I didn't see them, and they didn't recognize me; I didn't know them. I did have all their numbers; I knew where to telephone, where to get in touch with them. But instead of doing it, I sat down on a bench in the waiting area, and I was still there at seven-thirty in the evening. In the middle of the afternoon I had a cup of coffee . . . and spilled it on my skirt; it was *café au lait,* or cappuccini, rather.

X.G. *Yes, a cappuccino.*

M.D. Cappuccino. My skirt was white, and with the coffee on the white skirt, I was . . . well, it was disgusting. But I didn't even rinse off the skirt; I just stayed that way. I went back to my seat—exactly the same seat, it hadn't been taken—at the end of the bench. And I watched the people until seven-thirty in the evening, seven and a half hours in a row. Then, at seven-thirty, someone said, "It's seven-thirty." I watched night fall and I told myself, "All right, I'm really going to have to get moving," and that's when l called the producer, who was scared to death. There had been a plane crash north of Milan during the day. So there was a panic, a double panic, since people were afraid that I'd been on that plane, that I would have absentmindedly taken it instead of the one for Rome. I remember people in Paris drank champagne and said, "She isn't . . . she wasn't on that plane that . . . she wasn't in the plane that smashed." But then afterward, when I told all this, people were afraid because they said it was suicidal. But I felt really fine on that bench. That's what's a little bit . . . was a little bit dangerous. I was right where I was supposed to be. Nobody knew where I was. *Nobody* in the world.

X.G. *And why were they frightened, do you think?*

M.D. Well, it's just that I didn't want to go on; I didn't want to live anymore that day; that happens. Doesn't it?

X.G. *Yes.*

M.D. So it's something like that, since I wanted—I wanted to send a telegram to my child to tell him that I loved him. But it didn't occur to me that it was a dangerous state to be in. I said to myself, "Say, what if I sent a telegram to . . . my son." Like that, like an idea . . . like, "Say, I think I'll eat a tangerine!"

X.G.   *But is that a state then that's similar to Lol. V. Stein's?*

M.D.   Those are states that frighten me, you see, states like that. On the road, sometimes, I'm afraid I won't remember how to drive a car. It happens very seldom. I get really frightened, so I go slowly. Well . . . yes, I go pretty slowly.[75]

X.G.   *Right.*

M.D.   Yes. That is, I know that some days I have to go slowly. People don't generally know this for themselves and they should. Some days you have to go slowly. But from . . . from that standpoint, I don't think I'm different from other people. The little difference is that if I feel like staying on the bench at the airport in Rome, I do it.

X.G.   *Right. And other people tell themselves, "It's not possible to stay here."*

M.D.   Other people would tell themselves, "But then . . . no, no, I have to act, I have to get out of here . . ." and I think that I had to stay.

X.G.   *Well, yes. Why call that . . .*

M.D.   Something happened, something was satisfied in that wait. Maybe an extreme need for solitude.

X.G.   *Yes. It was a kind of absence from the world and . . . were you thinking about something?*

M.D.   No. Well, you're always thinking about something, but it was going on pretty much at a distance.

X.G.   *It was also being absent from yourself, a little.*

M.D.   I'm laughing because I can still see the look on those producers' faces when they saw me. I was hardly fresh as a daisy, covered with *café au lait.* They said, *"That's* Duras? Well, so what'll we do with her?" They seemed pretty pissed. [*Laughter.*] They took me to a very nice hotel . . . near the . . . what's that little square called with the fountains, in Rome?

X.G.   *There are so many in Rome . . .*

M.D.   The most beautiful of all, with the rivers . . . There's the Nile . . .

X.G.   *Oh, that's the Piazza Navona.*

M.D.   Piazza Navona—to a very good hotel; people stared at me. Disgusting, I was just disgusting.

X.G. *Yes, but there, you see, social behavior comes into play that's very . . . not very important. So they stared at you . . . so what?*

M.D. No, I mean it was the comic side of the story. Because I couldn't justify myself: I could at least have gone to the restroom and gotten rid of the coffee stains. But there was still a refusal, a profound refusal . . .

X.G. *Yes.*

M.D. . . . just to keep going.

X.G. *The same refusal as Lol. V. Stein's?*

M.D. Maybe. I hadn't thought of that, yes.

X.G. *When they say she's sick, what's wrong with her? She refuses, she no longer moves, she doesn't think . . . she no longer wants to move or think or . . . or anything.*

M.D. Yes. That's true.

X.G. *That's all her sickness is; it's a refusal.*

M.D. And when they talk about women who aren't well, when men talk about women among themselves, about their wives, you often happen to hear them say in conversations, "She doesn't want to move anymore, something's really wrong, she stays in bed, she just lies there."

X.G. *"She's sick . . ."*

M.D. That means that someone who would be capable of doing what I've just told you, what happened to me at the Rome airport, would certainly be more stricken, stricken . . . outright, with a little . . . maybe a little . . . psychosis, and that I do it without being as stricken as most people would be in . . .

X.G. *Yes. I'd really like to think so.*

M.D. Do you see?

X.G. *Yes, quite. [Silence.] But isn't it also because you write?*

M.D. You mean that . . . that it comes out?

X.G. *Yes.*

M.D. Oh, certainly.

X.G. *It's clear that if it didn't come out of you, then . . . then all of that*

would be in you, you realize—Lol. V. Stein and Anne-Marie Stretter,
you would be all that.

M.D. Maybe I wouldn't have made it through.

X.G. *Really. So they're frightened of that—I don't know—Michèle, your*
family, might be frightened that you write that, whereas, in fact,
it's . . .

M.D. It's what I tell her all the time: there's nothing to be afraid of.

X.G. *. . . it's better that it gets out, probably.*

M.D. That is, she was frightened because she thinks that instead of . . .
talking with you, in fact, I'm with the people of the Ganges, much
farther away, and all that's like a diminishing of presence . . . she
says all the time, "You think she's here, and then . . ."

X.G. *But isn't that something that happens to everyone?*

M.D. I'm sure it does, absolutely sure. Everyone is elsewhere at the same
time.

X.G. *Yes.*

M.D. But this elsewhere is more or less important . . . I don't know what's
going on with those people [*who are passing in the street*].

X.G. *Well, I don't know, it's a car.* [Silence.] *But for you, what's different*
about what happens? No, one can't ask that question, because that's
just like saying: how does it happen that you write? One can't ask
that; one can't explain that—that is, why everyone is elsewhere . . .
for example, we dream.

M.D. Yes, but maybe . . . it's an elsewhere that is perhaps more public for
me, basically a real elsewhere. I'm in Calcutta with the people of the
Ganges—maybe that's the only difference, a total elsewhere—
whereas other people are maybe elsewhere in their own life. In an
elsewhere that's not completely imaginary, that they could still go to.
A woman can be in an elsewhere with a man she loves who's not
her husband or . . . in a dream of being dispossessed, but that's
something she's more or less lived, do you see?

X.G. *Yes, yes.*

M.D. Whereas for me, it's an elsewhere that has nothing, not a single common root with the present that I live in.

X.G. *Right, it's true. It's like a foreign world that inhabits you.*

M.D. Exactly. [*Silence.*] You, your fear of dogs, your pathological fear of dogs . . .

X.G. *You can say that again!*

M.D. . . . it's total blackness. Have you tried to figure it out?

X.G. *Sometimes I try a bit; I don't get anywhere. But what makes you think of that?*

M.D. Because that's an elsewhere too, one of fear.

X.G. *But then, it's totally unknown and never manages to . . .*

M.D. But which is fixed, that's especially it. You're tied to this post, the fear of dogs.

X.G. *Oh, yes.*

M.D. It doesn't budge.

X.G. *That's true.*

M.D. And certainly you could think that it's a whole . . . that it immobilizes a whole mental situation.

X.G. *Yes.*

M.D. That if it . . . you could manage to see into it clearly, that . . . that it would move around, you understand?

X.G. *Yes, yes, yes, oh, that's clear, it would pull in a bunch of things. That's obvious. But there's also the fact that it just doesn't . . . that it can't take effect and then go out in . . . in just any old way. For example, your . . .*

[End of the tape. We don't notice it until too late. We try to get back what was lost.]

M.D. Is it working?

X.G. *Yes, yes.*

M.D. Yes, I was saying, you see, when I was twelve, thirteen, fourteen, fifteen, even sixteen years old, I would leave Sadec and . . . Vinh-long, the small posts of Cochin China, to go into . . . toward Kampot, where the Pacific dam was, and I went eight hundred kilometers like that with a little Indochinese driver, to go pay the workers. Well, we used to stop in the forest at the watering place, near the well, to drink, to put water in the motor; and there were always lepers near those wells. I began to have a phobia about leprosy, an anxiety about leprosy. Oh, I had that, I don't know, maybe two or three years; it lasted even after my . . . after the university; it came back at certain moments, a terrible fear of having gotten leprosy. I'd watch my sun spots, I'd see if they hurt. I remember one spot that I had on my arm—I thought it was a [*inaudible word*], you know, the first white spots. But it was a sun spot, no problem. So now, leprosy is in my books, and I'm not afraid of it at all anymore. The fear has completely passed, but it's as if what was holding me prisoner, bound to this pole of my fear, what caused the . . . the . . . the cord to break so that leprosy could spread into my books, that's what cured me of the fear; it's a therapy, fundamentally . . . I don't think we said anything else.

X.G. *Yes, we did. You also said that leprosy was not just leprosy, it was . . .*

M.D. That's right, yes, leprosy and all it brings along with it, hunger—I knew very, very early that leprosy came from eating only one kind of thing—famine, colonialism, lepers wandering in the forest of the Elephant Chain, and so on. It's become a whole backdrop; leprosy has become the light, if you like, of the colonialist backdrop where I spent my childhood.

X.G. *Yes.*

M.D. I don't think there was anything else.

X.G. *No, that was all.*

M.D. Yes, I was telling you that if you could burst open the link between your fear of dogs and . . . and dogs, it would spread out in you, in things you wouldn't suspect.

X.G. *Yes.*

M.D. It was a word I hardly dared pronounce when I was little: "leprosy." Now I write it. Because I remember my mother had a friend who had a baby; the baby had a Chinese nanny and . . . one day the . . . the nanny went for a checkup and the doctor—I remember this story because it was so spectacular—pierced her calf with a knitting

needle without her seeing it (she was looking out the window), and
the woman didn't even flinch. I was weaned on stories like that, you
see. I already knew all this when I was around seven, five years old.

X.G. *But I don't get it. Was it because he did acupuncture?*

M.D. No, no, because leprosy isn't painful; you don't feel anything.

X.G. *Ah!*

M.D. He wanted to prove to her employer that she had leprosy. She was
really fond of the nanny; it was something like that. He ran a very,
very fine steel needle through her calf. She didn't flinch.

X.G. *It's not painful . . . it's more than not painful; it's anesthetizing.*

M.D. It's anesthetizing. All that to say that this fear was our daily bread
there.

X.G. *But still it's funny, the play . . . um, the role it plays in your books.*

M.D. Well, it's absolute horror.

X.G. *Even more in "Indiana Song," don't you think?*

M.D. It's absolute horror.

X.G. *It's horror and at the same time, when the vice-consul says, "I'm not
at all afraid of catching it—on the contrary," I don't know, I think
there's a fascination, isn't there? What is it about horror? Because
if you throw yourself . . .*

M.D. It's the concretization of a horror. It's the furthest point; you can't go
any further.

X.G. *And that he prefers to throw himself into it.*

M.D. Oh, the vice-consul?

X.G. *Yes.*

M.D. Yes, there too, well, I have to say the word "religious" there's a desire
in the bones . . . osmotic, almost to . . . dissolve oneself in India.
Not in the India of the maharajas but in the India of . . . almost
caricatured, of leprosy and hunger.

X.G. *Yes.*

M.D. Leprosy is wandering, too, you see? Since they're outside the
villages . . . they *were:* now they're in camps.

X.G. *It's banishment; they're banished, outside. They're . . .*

M.D. Yes, and he too is banished, the vice-consul.

X.G.   *. . . outlawed, outside of society. Yes. But if it were religious, it would be a . . . like atoning for sins—I don't really know what—it would be like a sacrifice or like a . . . Oh no, that's not it.*

M.D.   No, not at all.

X.G.   *No. But then it's not religious.*

M.D.   Maybe it's in order not to feel it anymore, entering within it.

X.G.   *Yes.*

M.D.   Maybe the same as with fear, as with my fear. This *difference* between the lepers and you, to fill it in like that. Oh no, because if it's religious, that would be sharing the pain.

X.G.   *But that's it.*

M.D.   It's stupid, because you don't take away anything. You don't take any part of the leprosy away by entering into it; you add to it.

X.G.   *Well, it's pretty serious, to think that.*

M.D.   No, there it's more . . . religious; the religious movement is the movement toward the other . . . to get out of yourself, if you will, to dissolve within.

X.G.   *But why call it "religious" then?*

M.D.   Well, I can hardly see any other term, for it, for . . . to qualify that *élan,* that surge of the human being toward the whole. What would you call it?

X.G.   *Well . . . I don't know. It's a surge . . .*

M.D.   This erasing-out of the being in favor of the whole, which is a constant movement in . . . in those texts. It certainly has to be called some . . . in some way.

X.G.   *I don't know.*

M.D.   Where does it come from, the word "religious"?

X.G.   *I don't know. In any event, in religion, when you go toward someone else, it's by a concerted movement; you think it's good to do that.*

M.D.   It's a moral standard, but in this case it's terrible.

X.G.   *Whereas here . . . there's no erasure within the religion. On the contrary, he goes toward the other, and he's all that much happier.*

M.D.   On the contrary. Yes, that's it. And he wins his salvation. It's a frightful commerce, abominable, and as long as this commerce exists . . .

X.G. *He exists that much more . . .*

M.D. . . . as long as Christians are not detached from God, it will be disgusting . . . from their salvation . . .

X.G. *. . . that is, from themselves, or at least from the completely paranoid way they see themselves. That is, to be . . .*

M.D. But there, it must be for totally personal reasons of tolerability . . .

X.G. *What?*

M.D. . . . that he wants to dissolve.

X.G. *In other words, he can't avoid it, can't do otherwise; he doesn't choose either to . . . to do that.*

M.D. You see, the sick mother, the mother of a sick, retarded child, takes on the language of the retarded child; she becomes retarded herself in order to be closer to her child and to bear the situation.

X.G. *Yes.*

M.D. There's something about it that's . . . that's common and natural. Those who live the . . . in the poorest way are those Whites who live cloistered, far away from leprosy, separated from it.

X.G. *Protected.*

M.D. Yes.

X.G. *Like, for example, by the wire netting. Wire netting protects them from sharks, but it also protects them from lepers.*

M.D. Yes, from their begging.

X.G. *Say, maybe we should talk about the beggar woman. I don't know what . . . She's a fascinating character, the same way as Anne-Marie Stretter—in fact, you've said it: they're the same woman.*

M.D. She was already in *Le Barrage contre le Pacifique,* twenty years ago.

X.G. *Yes.*

M.D. It's very difficult to express, what you've just said. There's a very precise kind of wandering for the beggar woman that's marked off by names, through Siam—Laos first, Cambodia, Siam, Burma.

X.G. *Across thousands of kilometers.*

M.D.   Three or four thousand, maybe more; she goes down the river in Burma—what's it called? that passes through Rangoon—the Irrawaddy, she comes from Tonle-Sap. In fact, in *Le Vice-consul*, I have her come upriver toward the Cardamoms.

X.G.   *But up to where? Until . . .*

M.D.   Until she ruins herself in Calcutta, but she ruins herself, she dissolves in Calcutta. I'm really afraid that the word "ruin" will be badly . . . be misunderstood. She is set on fire in Calcutta just as the vice-consul is consumed by leprosy.

X.G.   *Yes.*

M.D.   As Anne-Marie Stretter is consumed with her, the beggar woman, that is by . . . by hunger, by pain. All that ends in a single chunk.

X.G.   *Yes.*

M.D.   She—Anne-Marie Stretter—has been wandering around in the capitals of Asia for seventeen years.

X.G.   *Until she can find, as you say, a direction for losing herself.*

M.D.   Exactly.

X.G.   *And then, when she's totally lost, that's when . . .*

M.D.   . . . whereas the beggar woman lives in daily joy.

X.G.   *Yes, but she's lost.*

M.D.   She's completely lost.

X.G.   *She lives on that loss.*

M.D.   She lives on that loss. [*Silence.*] It's completely equivalent.

X.G.   *Yes.*

M.D.   Anne-Marie Stretter's disappearance and the survival of the beggar. They blend together.

X.G.   *I see them doing practically the same movements, the same . . . Do you see?*

M.D.   Yes.

X.G.   *Yet they're completely different, since one wears the rags of the embassy and the other the rags of the beggar, but in spite of everything, I see them as being very much the same.*

M.D.   That's going to really shock the imbeciles out there, isn't it?

X.G. *It will shock them? Oh, maybe, yes.*

M.D. How can one dare make a parallel between a begging seen as sacred by all the moral . . .

X.G. *Yes, it's true. I hadn't even thought about that.*

M.D. . . . and the wife of an ambassador of France?

X.G. *Well, listen, as far as that goes, too bad for them if that's the point they're at!*

M.D. Oh well, you know . . .

X.G. *But okay, we have to try to figure out how the movement is similar and is almost love between the two, finally, it seems to me, without their knowing each other, you see, and how . . . and why it's different because, for example, one needs to kill herself and the other doesn't.*

M.D. The one who doesn't need to—there's a self-sufficiency in the beggar woman; it's enough for her to walk, to sleep, to swim in the Ganges in order to catch fish, to sing the Savannakhet song in order to dance. She's still liberated, though she's living death.

X.G. *Yes.*

M.D. It's exactly that. Living, she's dead.

X.G. *And Anne-Marie Stretter needs to kill herself.*

M.D. I'm thinking. She can't do anything else anymore, I believe.

X.G. *You know, it's strange because . . . I wouldn't even say that she kills herself; I would say that she gives herself to death.*

M.D. That's perfect, yes.

X.G. *That she delivers herself to it, that it's a completion. Do you think you could say that the beggar woman, that it's her Indian culture that . . .*

M.D. Very good; it's just the opposite.

X.G. *. . . that permits her to live like that, being dead, whereas Anne-Marie Stretter doesn't have that?*

M.D. That's it totally; I really like that, yes.

X.G. *And then also the difference, still . . . it's the same; Anne-Marie Stretter and the vice-consul are very close, even more than close . . .*

M.D. They're the same.

x.g. *Well, all right then, yet how does it happen that Anne-Marie Stretter . . . can identify somewhat with a beggar woman of the Ganges and that the vice-consul, for his part, his proximity to the lepers is to shoot at them? I don't know how to say it, there's a difference . . .*

M.D. There's already a link of passion there with the leprosy.

x.g. *To shoot at them.*

M.D. Yes.

x.g. *Yes. But Anne-Marie Stretter also has a link of passion with the pain of India.*

M.D. Yes.

x.g. *But it's not the same. She can't shoot at the lepers.*

M.D. No.

x.g. *I would really like to define this; I don't know how we can know . . .*

M.D. Anne-Marie Stretter is in the world of desire . . .

x.g. *But the vice-consul—it's certainly his desire, too.*

M.D. . . . but in a satisfied desire. The vice-consul is a virgin.

x.g. *Yes. Yes.*

M.D. Anne-Marie Stretter is desire.

x.g. *Yes. And that allows her, that allows her a fusion.*

M.D. Ah, yes.

x.g. *A relinquishment to the pain of India, like a relinquishment to death.*

M.D. Yes.

x.g. *The vice-consul can't.*

M.D. It's always the outside-of-self, the voice outside-of-self.

x.g. *Yes.*

M.D. Desire is the biggest voice.

x.g. *Yes.*

M.D. So the pain, all that, is very, very, very close.

x.g. *Yes.*

M.D. I think that it's a generalized thought, if you will, that inhabits the vice-consul.

x.g. *How do you mean?*

M.D.   He's like a walking book. He hardly has any life. Do you see?

X.G.   *Yes.*

M.D.   It's bloodless in him; it's the generalized idea. It says, "What was it he couldn't stand? The idea."

X.G.   *Yes.*

M.D.   The idea of India. He's also shooting at principles, at philosophies, when he fires. That's the opening toward the sensory world. Toward desire, that's what it is.

X.G.   *But it's an opening that can only lead toward nothing, that can't lead.*

M.D.   Yes. Furthermore, the vice-consul disappears. He is obliterated, at the end; after her death he gives his resignation, and all trace of him disappears. We don't know what happened to him. He's exploded.

X.G.   *So he disappears like the lepers disappear.*

M.D.   Exactly. Absolutely.

X.G.   *Like sacks of dust, you say. That's fascinating, this . . . how everyone in their own way goes back to leprosy.*

M.D.   It's mysterious to me too. I see movements, but I see them already in motion; I don't . . . I don't ever say, "I'm going to have him do this to express that." It's after the fact and when people ask me questions that I make an effort. I always say what I've said to you; "I find the madmen of S. Thala on the beach. I don't know how they got there." It's taking place somewhere but . . . it's other people who know how it began. It's others, maybe, who have inside them the beginning of that. Why wouldn't things be fragmented in people?

X.G.   *And how would it come to you?*

M.D.   Well, I happened to be on the road to . . . just like that, one day, without my knowing it. I have this idea. It seems loony, what I'm telling you, but I . . .

X.G.   *I don't know, I'm hesitating between acknowledging something very true and something . . .*

M.D.   Artificial.

X.G.   *Bizarre, you see, a kind of . . . I don't know, of magic.*

M.D.   Yes, you're saying that you can't quite believe that it doesn't exist, that you're completely in the imaginary world. I don't quite want to believe it, and it's . . . it would be wrong to believe that I invented the story alone.

X.G. *Yes.*

M.D. If I were alone in the world, the story wouldn't have come to me.

X.G. *Oh no, that's certainly true.*

M.D. Then it must have come out of a . . . it was somewhere inhabiting others, that story.

X.G. *Yes, yes, there now, put like that I understand it really well, yes.*

M.D. Isn't it so? That there are people whom I was near, whom I knew, who gave me this, that, and the other thing until the story was fabricated. But I draw it out of you; I draw it out of others. That's why I can tell you that maybe it's others who have the beginning of the story in their possession. The writers who think they're alone in the world, even some great writers—that's all monstrous damned stupidity.

X.G. *Of course. Oh, yes, what you're saying is really good.*

M.D. I make my books with others. The transformation that it undergoes may be a little strange, the sound that it makes when it passes through me, but that's all. It's a sound that it makes when it passes through somebody it's given to.

X.G. *But it's funny about that, because what you're saying is like the scene in "Indiana Song"; it makes a sound as it appears on stage.*

M.D. Well, yes, exactly. Maybe I'm just an echo-chamber. It isn't out of modesty that I say this; I really believe it.

X.G. *Yes, yes.*

M.D. Really.

X.G. *Would you like a cigarette?*

M.D. I think I'll have a little wine. They're going to say, "She's drinking again, that Duras!" [*Laughter. Sound of glasses and liquid.*]

X.G. *You see, I'm having some wine too.*

M.D. I think we can stop here, can't we?

X.G. *Yes.*

M.D. That will be the most important thing, what I've just said.

Notes

1 Translator: For the sake of consistency, I have kept all book and movie titles
 in these interviews in French, whether by Duras or by others. (For a list of
 Duras's corresponding English translations, please refer to the bibliography.)
 All translations are mine.

 I would like to express my deepest thanks to Margaret Waller and Alice
 Jardine for their expert editing, to Danielle Haase Dubose, Amy Cohen, and
 Claude Samerd for their assistance with French idioms, and to Marcelle
 Marini and Nancy K. Miller for providing essential information on the
 context of these interviews and suggestions for the shape of the Afterword.

2 x.g. Instead of *blanc,* I had typed by mistake *blance.* (Translator: *Blance* is
 not a word in French but Gauthier may have been amalgamating *blanc,*
 "blank," and *béance,* "gaping".)

3 x.g. "During her illness, she said her name in anger." What is also extremely
 troubling is that while she's making love, she designates herself by her own
 name *and* by that of Tatiana Karl, her friend.

4 x.g. Instead of *la loi* (the law), I had typed *le loi.* (Translator: Gauthier typed
 a masculine definite article where a feminine article should be.)

5 x.g. And where, then, can we account for the female homosexual?

6 x.g. I don't trust the kind of fascination that the androgyne exerts. I see it as
 a negation of woman. She's barely emerging into history, and already people

163

say: "Men and women are the same; there's no longer any difference; there are no longer men and women." We've got unisex clothes, angels' clothes, sexless. And into this angel, woman, having barely appeared, disappears.

7   x.g. This sentence is ridiculous and dangerous. I'm talking here exactly like the men who have always told women what they were. Here I am in full feminist mimeticism. All I could have said was: "They don't like to hear women say what women are."

8   x.g. You'd think I was talking about a divine grace! What I mean is something like a confrontation, a test, a serious one, which you were lucky enough to fail and which then permitted a loss, a death to a certain kind of system, a gaping that you know to be incurable . . .

9   x.g. I don't understand this passage at all (or the next five pages). I don't know what fidelity, adultery, and so on, mean. I especially don't understand how I could let myself get caught up in speaking about (and in seeming to agree with) this pseudo-contradiction between making love and loving, based on a dualist, objectivist philosophy that divides the body and soul!

M.D. Linguistic terror is not something I'm familiar with. Already, in *Détruire, dit-elle*, I had proposed in principle this equivalence between desire and love ("Love, desire, they're the same thing," says Stein or Alissa, I don't remember). And if you read through, it circulates pretty much on the quiet in all my writings. Right now, on this issue, I'm not speaking for myself. I'm speaking for women other than ourselves. Here we're at the very center of woman's paralysis, maybe even more than in that other place of dualism—abortion. On the other hand, to refuse to talk about it because it doesn't concern you is false. You see, I believe we're still much closer to the millions of Muslim women who are "dishonored," beaten, punished, sometimes killed, because they betrayed their husbands than to the most liberal European husband. To talk to these women about the dualism you're denouncing makes them smile, the same as it does their husbands. I believe that there's nothing, nothing more anchored than that dualism, in all of us—and in you and me. When you say, "I don't understand what the words fidelity, adultery mean," I'm sorry, but I think you're lying to yourself. You understand those words. I understand them. When I propose the equivalence Stein talks about in *Détruire,* I propose it based on a life lived in complete contradiction to it. It's as if you said to me, "I've freed myself of Christianity," to say you live this equivalence. We know what the words "fidelity" and "adultery" mean. I have *betrayed* in horror, passion, despair, guilt, and all that. When people say to women, "Go ahead, sleep with anyone you like; it's not betraying the husband, the lover, to sleep with another man," that's a complete lie and it's idiotic. To sleep with another man is to betray the husband or lover if there's desire *both* for the other man *and* the husband or lover: it's desire itself that has *mistaken* the body, that *betrays*. Or else it's a question of those bleak and sterile experiments "for the principle of it" that women who want to get out of the paralysis of a senseless fidelity commit themselves to. In which case, there's no betrayal; there isn't anything, anywhere. And the women who commit themselves to such tests don't get free of the paralysis; they sink themselves into it more deeply. The example that free couples present often coincides with the absence of desire. They're false couples; there's an impressive number of them—both now and in the past. Let's speak without taboos, but let's be careful, because this linguistic space is the trickiest place there is. This equivalence we're talking about isn't just words we're offering; if we find it, it's because it's been lived, because we've lived it; to deny it would be a lie of reactionary proportions. Yes, desire lived at the brothel, the "I love you" said with closed eyes to the whores is of the same *nature* as what is lived in the passion for one single person, what is generally called passion. In every case, we're declaring our love to love itself. But what does that mean actually? It means that we know, from the moment we live it, that this equivalence carries in itself or is by itself, whichever you like, its own end. And that it's in its nature to be contradictory to itself, to express at the same time the generality of desire, the circulation of desire, and its brutal fastening. So it happens that this equivalence doesn't let go and that it seems to express a brutal *choice.* If it no longer disembeds itself from a choice, from its contradiction, then you get to that blazing absurdity of passion, and then to fidelity, but one that's organically decreed, so that you can no longer betray the object of passion that has been designated for you without horror. You could think here of the drug addict's horror when he needs a fix and is given a substitute for his drug. So you see, at the very place of this equivalence's blossoming, we come back to this fidelity—inevitably—which you qualify as nonsense. This alienation is desirable to the utmost you can live it. No, I don't see anything of any nature whatsoever more desirable than to live it. But if you haven't lived it, what I'm saying must be unacceptable, necessarily.

X.G. I understand better and recognize that what I wrote seemed a bit like a proclamation-declaration . . . but for me, what you say doesn't seem to take into account the desire-passion of a woman for another woman. And the ambiguity of a desire that can attach itself to a man by passing through a woman or to a woman by passing through a man. On the contrary, this seems to me to appear in your works with a rare violence.

M.D. If I have lived it, and probably I have, it's all escaped from me. I've known desire-passion for several women. It's never been further than the first times. The man's frustration always swept everything aside, and very soon, I would leave the woman to come back to be with men. Once, during a trip with a woman, I left her in the middle of the trip to come back to Paris. Yet I find woman's body more beautiful in its nudity than man's body, more desirable also, but the woman brings me an orgasm that's not dizzying; it's like the child's.

10   M.D. But still, it's not the same frigidity. No. *Jouissance* isn't the body; it's orgasm. Between no orgasm at all and a mechanical orgasm there is an essential distinction. The pleasure of the body with no orgasm—I don't understand what that means.

X.G. But there can be an orgasm without *jouissance,* I mean without true *jouissance* of the body, of the whole body.

11   M.D. I think we should stop lying to ourselves about this. Suppressed adultery, suppressed clandestine love, like all lost clandestine things, represents, at the same time that it's desirable, represents a loss—somewhere. I don't like it when people say: "Everything's bad; it all has to be thrown away and nothing regretted." I regret even as I throw away.

12   "Man must cease being a *theoretical imbecile.* The great alignment brought

about the world over by young people, over the minimum condition of the human being (of which the female condition and then the working condition are the first aspect) implies the abandonment, by man, of his theoretic prattle and his access to the silence common to all oppressed peoples.

"Man must learn to be quiet, which is probably something very painful for him. To silence the theoretical voice in himself, the practice of theoretical interpretation. *He has to heal himself.* We don't even have the time to live out an event as momentous as May 1968 before man begins to speak, moves to theoretical epilogue and breaks the silence. Yes, this chatterer made still more converts in May 1968. He's the one who began to speak again and to speak alone and *for* everyone, *in the name* of everyone, as he put it. Immediately, he silenced women and the mad; he set the ancient language rolling, he solicited the *ancient theoretical* practice in order to speak, recount, explain this *new* phenomenon: May 1968.

"He played the theoretical cop, and that silent, enormous brouhaha that rose from the crowd—*the silence here was precisely the sum of all the voices,* equaling the sum of all our breathing—he put a muzzle on it.

"He was afraid, deep down, that he had been lost; suddenly he had no grandstand anymore, and he hooked back onto the ancient discourse; he called it to his aid. There's been no silence since May '68. And this collective silence was necessary because it would have been in this silence that a new way of being could have been stirred up; it would have been in the mutual obscurity that collective ways of behaving would have pierced through, found inroads.

"No, man had to break everything and *stop the course of silence*" (Marguerite Duras in Suzanne Hover and Janne Socquet, *La Création étouffée,* ed. Pierre Horay).

13 x.g. In *Marguerite Duras* by Alain Vircondelet.

14 Translator: Henry de Montherlant (1896–1972) was an existentialist novelist and playwright whose works represent life as inherently meaningless and thereby justify the individual's self-interest; all social acts in a meaningless,

167

amoral universe are calculated, one way or another, to provide personal gratification and are motivated by hubris.

15 X.G. It's not the opposite: that would be the antihero, thus the same mechanism. This is a destruction, an annihilation of that very notion.

16 Translator: In French the verb *ravir* has several meanings, all of which enter into Duras's use of the word (cf. *Le Ravissement de Lol. V. Stein*). It means to ravish, to kidnap, to abduct; to rob somebody of/from something or somebody; it also means to delight.

17 M.D. But it's almost he each time. This adverb "almost," what is it? It takes the Scholastic entity down a peg. Have you ever been waiting for someone in a public place, a railroad station, a cafe, waiting while watching the people pass by? Well then, you've had the experience of seeing *almost her, almost him,* with the slight difference that *they* don't know *you.* It's a thing I've thought a lot about. For me, the erotic link of the third person is this *almost.* But here, the *almost* is inside the *altogether* and dislodges me in turn. If it's *almost he,* then it's *almost I* who recognize him. What happens is always outside: who is ever completely, altogether, there?

18 M.D. No, it's not because it's unattainable or invented that it's Romanticism; it would be Romanticism if it really existed, I think.

19 M.D. In *India Song,* the vice-consul cries out his love for Anne-Marie Stretter in the streets of Calcutta; he cries out in a public place what is admitted only under one's breath.

20 M.D. I said all this in the "Notes" to *Nathalie Granger.* That is to say, I took up again in the book what I discovered in these interviews.

21 M.D. "Metaphysical" is a word that doesn't frighten me. There's the prefix "meta," the widest, and the word "physical."

22 X.G. After having seen the two films again, I no longer think quite this way. I saw, first, in *Nathalie Granger,* let's say, a "social" aspect, and here I enclosed it and reduced it considerably. Perhaps this was also a way to deal with the tension that the film had provoked in me.

23 Translator: There are 100 old francs in one new franc; Duras, therefore, was paid 10,000 new francs for her work on *Hiroshima*.

24 M.D. I have, according to my agent, 0.5 percent of the receipts. The contract was illegal. The law of March 11, 1957, provides for 0.5 percent *in all cases*. This law went into effect March 12, 1958, and the contract is dated July 1, 1958. After the film's release, I got a check for a million and some francs; I thought it was a "gesture" on the producer's part. (One of them had told me: "We owe you so much, we'll make a gesture.") This was not a gesture; it was the obligatory clause of March 11, 1958. I was so disgusted, I gave away that money. Ever since, each year I get something between 1,500 and 2,000 francs, because of this 0.5 percent.

Speaking of which, I don't know why Resnais said in his interview in *Le Monde* that I had phoned to make the film. He was the one who had Olga Wormser call me. I was completely unaware that he was making a film.

25 M.D. I have looked at the book: no, she answers, "At first, no, I don't cry out, I call you softly." Now, what I did earlier interests me more. They help me get away from being disgusted with myself sometimes, these traces that you leave behind and don't recognize most of the time.

26 M.D. These repetitions—I really have to apologize.

x.G. Perhaps, in any event, we should explain a bit (at the risk of creating a new repetition of the preface!). In the Second Interview, the one preceding this, we knew that we had lost a lot of spoken material, but what exactly? We had immediately tried to get it back. Since this Third Interview was made the day after the second, I hadn't had time to transcribe it, and we didn't know exactly what was in it. This repetition, then, is based on a double forgetfulness. We also must say that we never knew where we were going, that we never knew in advance what we would speak about, that we were completely "inside" of what we were doing.

27 M.D. It's not the word "waves" [*flots*]; I've never used that a single time in my life. What could it be? I have replaced it with the word "small islands" [*îlots*].

28 x.G. Instead of "maidservants" [*bonnes à tout faire*], a woman friend who

typed much of the text typed by mistake "manservants" [*hommes à tout faire*].

29 M.D. And would you talk about a wage for whores? I would. We're dealing with exactly the same matter: if you pay everybody's whore, you also pay the businessman's whore. I don't understand you. The same sale takes place, the same kind, with hypocrisy as well. So what?

X.G. So the hypocrisy changes everything. What man, what woman will recognize—as Simone de Beauvoir says, I think—that marriage is legalized prostitution? In the current demand of certain prostitutes to be paid by Eros Centers (and to be taxed!), there must be some kind of recognition that what they do is real labor (a demand, furthermore, that's rather frightening in that it only masks a bit more the incredible wretchedness of sexual relations).

30 M.D. It's the same thing.

X.G. No, it would only be because the employer, the boss, is the husband or the lover at the same time. And a laborer's wife, for example, who works a lot more (because she has more children and no maid, few electric household appliances, and so on) than the wife of a big bourgeois (who's got nothing to do but be there) will be much less "paid," because it's a question of her husband's wage. Now a wage is, in principle, proportionate to the work supplied.

31 M.D. After the Fascist putsch in Chile, in the anger we all shared, this is what I dreamed: it's morning in Santiago; Pinochet's tanks, the armed troops—all that is in place as usual, and the city is empty. No one's there anymore. In the night, the city was emptied out. There's no longer a single inhabitant. Santiago is a desert. And I see Pinochet and his tanks faced with this emptiness. Where are they? Gone.

32 M.D. Even for couples who say: "It's not the same for us; our house is open to everyone." They may be the worst, the ones who play this liberal comedy, because they even share in other people's cheating.

33 Translator: The French expression *se mettre ensemble,* for which there is no equivalent English term, means literally "to put or place themselves to-

gether." It therefore conveys a sense of mutual dependency in a couple, a doubled self-absorption.

34   Translator: Gauthier has shifted from the formal pronoun *vous,* which both women have been using to address one another in the interviews, to the informal *tu.* This shift to intimacy during the interview sessions clearly reflects the pronoun usage already in effect outside the recording periods.

35   X.G. *La Femme du Gange* is emptiness. The emptiness unarticulated and then articulated. Pure suffering and desire, pure of all emotion, of all sentiment, of all convolution. Suffering and desire, you could say, purged themselves of all suffering, of all desire.

36   X.G. The false recollection is also that of the madmen of S. Thala.

37   X.G. That will be *India Song.*

38   M.D. I also saw leprosy in the forest villages, around the wells, but never as much as in Singapore. Those islands, I can see them so well. *The Prince of Wales* was a hotel in Colombo, a port of call for the shipping companies.

39   X.G. I must say I'm a little ashamed in rereading that kind of passage! Why such gibberish when it would have been so simple to say: You left Asia to come to the West; in your books Anne-Marie Stretter leaves the beaches in the North to go toward India. It's an opposite path.

40   X.G. It's also the past of our Western culture. The future is the West that's going to swallow up everything and kill this ancient culture. But the past still remains, back there.

M.D. Something strange is that tune "Blue Moon," it travels through people's hearts, even of those who haven't ever heard it before. The past begins very young. At the age of twenty, there it is. Love, the memory of love, is there at age twenty. Someone said, "This is a film by an older director." And someone else said, "That's the biggest mistake. Memory is what begins earliest, before judgment, before everything." *Le Barrage contre le Pacifique* is the true book on memory, and I was less than thirty when I wrote it.

41   X.G. Such is the force of the group, the madness of the group, the force of

their death from inside their life. One of the most beautiful scenes, and nearly unbearable, shows the force of those who are lighting the fires. Their hands are black; they're in front of him, the one who thought he was still an individual, who had decided to find *his* past. He's annihilated, devoured by the collective force, which is anonymous, terrible, unaware of itself.

42   M.D. I don't like that word "organic" anymore. And yet it's appropriate.

43   M.D. I took that up again in the screenplay. I discovered that quite late: that she called them because . . . and so on.

44   M.D. The form that moves, that goes. When she's not following, she sleeps. It is said: "She has to sleep or she dies." I think she's still exhausted from the S. Thala ball, from that night. What she glimpsed that night—I see the light of lightning around it—was supposed to kill her. Unkilled, she continues to be animated by apparent life. Life functions, her legs, her eyes, her organs work, but only "accidentally," you could say. The accident here would be life (*I see* the Jews in Europe coming out alive after the last world war like "accidents," but of death, each one representing a breakdown in Hitler's death machine. Even now *I see* Israel with two times less the inhabitants than the population of dead Jews). She belongs to the four winds, exposed, this form of Lol. V. Stein. Anne-Marie Stretter, too, who belongs to whoever wants her: prostitute of Calcutta. L.V.S. and A.-M.S. join one another here, in this expropriation of themselves. But with A.-M.S., it's not conscious. For L.V.S., it is. The white. The black. The white sands of S. Thala where L.V.S. dissolves. The black, the black monsoon of Calcutta where Anne-Marie Stretter is "made." It's all the same. All my women. They are invaded by the outside, pervaded, shot through all over by desire. In the film, I really like the way the madmen take care of L.V.S.'s sleep; they make her walk, come home, sleep; they protect her life, the beating of her heart, her gaze, her steps. Around Anne-Marie Stretter, on the other hand, there's nothing except a lover, except the desert of one man's passion. But the trajectories of the shot-through bodies cross each other.

45   M.D. When people talk about *Nathalie Granger,* they're speaking about the film and its content, as it concerns other films, other contents. When they

speak about *La Femme du Gange,* I have the feeling that they remain inside the film.

46   x.g. It's the same filling up of the blanks, the empty spaces that there are in traditional writing.

47   x.g. She allows the traveler passage toward emptiness. His suffering finds a panicked, burning echo in her, not in Lol. V. Stein (or else it's just an echo that repeats mechanically, like an echo against a wall). The woman in black allows the traveler to sink himself in suffering. To sink in the literal sense of the term: he'll never come back from it; he'll never live his suffering any longer; he'll be drowned in *the* suffering (which is also that of the others).

48   m.d. They've often made me think of Albertine, L.V.S. and the second madman—a two-headed Albertine.

49   x.g. Marguerite Duras was saying that it's too bad there are different languages, that one should be able to write in a universal language that everyone could understand immediately. I said that would only be a monopoly, an American-Western imperialism.

m.d. Yes, it seems that it was a crime against linguistics. I said that to be a Greek, Bulgarian, Swedish poet, and so on, must be terrible. I also said what a Swedish poet told me about the Swedish translation of *Fleurs du mal:* among them all, there were maybe two that were translatable, that you could consider as translated; the rest were impossible to do.

50   Translator: *Bac, (baccalauréat)* is a major examination in the French secondary educational system giving university entrance qualification. *Philo, (philosophie),* which Duras mentions later, is a program of study of philosophy and the arts.

51   m.d. No, I don't believe in this double culture; I mean in its influence, its resurgence. For that matter, how could I answer with a yes or no?

52   Translator: In *Le Barrage contre le Pacifique.*

53   x.g. How could they get the missing piastre?

m.d. Sometimes they would sell their sampan.

54 M.D. *Racs* (I don't remember how it's spelled) are the small floods that come straight down from the mountain, from the Elephant Chain. After storms, they carry along broken trees and drowned animals.

55 X.G. The film is afterward. After the invasion, when there's nothing left of the bragging, vengeful West except sand. In the same way that there's nothing left of men's aggression except some madmen and madwomen who know what they're doing all the better because their acts have no sense.

M.D. Yes. But still I don't see the people in S. Thala *standing out* against anything at all, even against a distant background of a capitalist society, or of colonialism, and so on. They're in a dead point in space, a dead point in time. There's no more process. It's not against an order of things or an ideology that S. Thala exists. I see plenitude attained at the place where the sands are, but precisely, in the suspension itself, in the very emptying of what's animal. The wait for the future is serene, but it's a violent serenity. They look ahead, they march ahead, toward "the Open" that Rilke talks about, which we "know only through the face of the animal." Only the woman in black drags along in herself a "sly" region, one that's nostalgic, painful. For the others, that's all over, and no coercive force, no enticement, can make them come back, because there's no more path to come back on; it was erased (the paths in the sand that are erased in the wind). And this is, at the same time, absolute political loss, for capitalist society I mean. And also maybe absolute political gain: they *are* politics; they don't *practice* politics anymore.

56 X.G. In my opinion, what's over—at least, you have to struggle so that what remains gets finished off—is Romanticism (idealism) which is, in effect, the product of a certain class, of certain class relations. But for me, your texts and films aren't about that at all. Passions there are so totally stripped of their sugary coating, their psychological explanations. What came about is the product of a certain economy of desire at the same time that there's a disintegration—it's visible in what you do—of what supports these "psychological" rapports: bourgeois society.

57 M.D. Every time you ask me that question I slip away; I run off into memories of childhood. I can only stand myself anymore in the *concrete*. Each incursion into generalizations makes me uneasy, as if I'd started lying

again, the way I used to lie in "society" before, or at the university.

58   M.D. This is grotesque, ridiculous, what I'm saying about the Buddhist monks, *now*. And it's false. Those walks into the mountain fascinated and terrified me—I remember suddenly—because I thought that access to the monasteries was forbidden. I believed the monks were dangerous because gifted with supernatural powers—my brother said so. It's *now* that I say: "It was beautiful." So I'm lying. It wasn't beautiful; it was something fantastic (in the literal sense). We used to hide to watch the forbidden performance. I let myself go in the ritual of evocation (of the childhood memory). If I told you: "On the beach, the sand, there were sometimes tracks of tigers," that's already more important.

59   M.D. Or rather, the man who is doubled by a Marxist conscience. The man who would in himself have nothing but a Marxist conscience, who would want himself to be like that every minute of his life—the simplified man, in short—is the model proposed in principle by Stalinism. This is a dangerous, terrifying man. This simplification of man was Hitlerism; it's Stalinism. All simplification is Fascist (in the army, religious orders, the police). Hitlerism and Stalinism meet here. The Hitler informer who "does his job," and Marchais who goes on television to say that Solzhenitsyn is a traitor, and the Soviet soldier who enters Prague and who, in the same way, "does his job"— they are all men of a single conscious, *simplified*. And all things considered, this white and sleek and "atypical" illness of the Party member, of the son above reproach, is because he's already entered into the simplification. The Left that they call "deviant" should in my opinion be lived as the safeguard against this danger. The mania for militancy is such that the leftists would like to change that inalienableness there—outside—into a further militancy, a derived ideology. That's naive. To anchor the Left is to make it disappear and to bring another into being later on. Every revolutionary man is his own leftist. The true Communist will always have inside him the wild place of his own contradiction, always ready for exploration. It's the place of his disorder, of his refusal, his double place, which will always reappear later on, more solid, if ever he is besieged by indoctrination and dislodged *from the inside which is his place*. If the Chinese don't understand that, don't admit it, if

175

they too believe that everything's reducible in man, well then, all revolution is doomed.

60   M.D. Again, it's about that breakdown in revolutionary action that we've seen since May 1968. Again, the more or less general knowledge that the proletariat has about the exact terms of its exploitation by capitalism aren't sufficient enough to move it into revolutionary action. That's the worker's schizophrenia. He knows, but that's not enough. For him to move into action, there has to be something more than this knowledge. In 1917 that was enough. But it isn't at all anymore. It's not just that he has before his eyes the huge betrayal of socialism that Soviet Russia represents. Nor that the Communist parties obedient to Stalin have done everything in the last twenty to thirty years to slow up, to blacken, to infantilize revolutionary action and the revolutionary idea—all this on Moscow's orders. It's still something more than that. What? Maybe it's that Marxism, given the very fact that it lends itself to such distortions and betrayals, has lost a little of its obviously dazzling worth, has lost a little of its poetic worth (and that's what's most serious). Yes, maybe we have to look toward the aging of Marxist consciousness and its now secular standstill. Writers the world over, whoever they may be, compose out of Marxism. And each writer who talks about it is convinced that it's he who, finally, holds the true key to dreams. Marxist knowledge has been sucked into the heritage of general culture and has already begun to take on a cadaverous stiffness. Like Freudianism. But perhaps also this immobile proletariat, with its occasional cries, is submerged especially in fantastic phraseology, with people speaking for it on every side; we don't realize, it seems to me, to what extent theoretical speech *separates*, brings about segregation. It has already separated women, that's certain. And now maybe it's separating the proletariat. The same militant Marxists who say: "At school, the child doesn't have enough initiative; he's been too muzzled," these are the same ones who call for major reforms in teaching, who militate like their grandfathers and who, when there are strikes or political meetings, run as fast as they can to talk and to explain for hours and hours to the workers the *political meaning* of their action. I can't go to this kind of meeting at all anymore, it's impossible.

61   X.G. Because it's not about a knowledge but about a practice.

62   Translator: Maurice Druon, writer and member of the Académie Française, is a man with rightist politics.

63   X.G. No, militancy is to carry the "good word" to the outside, to preach it to others, maybe without having analyzed anything, having discovered nothing in oneself.

     M.D. Or the example.

64   X.G. All this said in complete naiveté—in complete forgetfulness that what we're saying could be read by hundreds of men!

65   X.G. I wonder why I said that? Maybe because I was thinking about the conversation we were alluding to.

66   Translator: In French, "death" is *la mort*, "love" is *l'amour*. Duras's assimilation of the terms, in addition to whatever connotative value it has, shows a homophonic logic.

67   "[M. Duras] quickly falls back into her own universe, which, since *Moderato cantabile*, can be easily reduced to the wound of love. A painter of instinctual women, brought down by passion, and who, once bruised, aggravate their wounds by facilitating infidelity or by being involved in it . . . How far away she is from Colette and her healthiness, her balance, her lucidity, her enthusiasm for life, animals, nature!"

     X.G. When I saw her (regarding the interviews I spoke about in the preface), she said to me: "Duras—no one knows what she writes; it's not literature. It's like her films; they're not cinema . . .

     M.D. Oh, I really like that!

68   Translator: Saint-Cyr is a military school founded in 1808, near Versailles.

69   M.D. In fact, the definitive title will be *India Song*.

70   M.D. I said, ". . . as if there were someone responsible." As if. And the word

"religious" doesn't shock me. Nor the word "God." It's the word "religion" that shocks me. To use the word "God" seems to me less serious than to use the word "reality."

All my life, even when I was small, I've seen life's appearance on earth in this form: a gigantic and inert marsh on whose surface, suddenly, an air bubble bursts, a single one, stinking; then—thousands of years pass—another one bursts. At the same time that these air bubbles, these life bubbles, manage to free themselves from the bottom of the marsh, the light is changing, the moisture lifts and light comes to the surface of the waters. For me the waters in Genesis were like that: heavy, weighty as liquid steel, but cloudy, under fog, deprived of light. The first noise is the bursting of the bubble, reverberating to "infinity." God was totally absent from my first landscape. And yet, when I read Genesis, I also read the word "God," but as an other: "the Spirit of God," for me, was the nauseating contents of the exploded bubbles. But these first exhalations were not provoked from the outside by a god's decree. I saw the light just as independent of everything; it had come from an elsewhere, from a material unknown, from an innocent *before-anything*. In this childhood polytheism, God had a precise place: he was the air inside the bubble. But he hadn't made the bubble. Nor the light. Nor the waters. Nor me. And all this, like the contents of the bubble, was the life yet to come. I've never believed in God, never, even as a child. And, even as a child, I've always seen believers as victims of a kind of spiritual infirmity, a kind of irresponsibility. When I was older and read Spinoza, Pascal, Ruysbroeck, I saw the faith of mystics as a despair of nonbelief. I continue to see them this way, absolutely, completely. They shriek of nonbelief. When I had my baby, I thought I was going through an anti-clerical crisis because I chased away the sisters who came near my son's stroller to ooh and ah, "Oh, the beautiful baby!" But it wasn't even a crisis. It was just the expression of violent physical disgust that Christians have always brought out in me. I didn't want that blackness to come near my child, that filth inherent in the believer's body which, as a child (and maybe even still) I felt knew neither sexual pleasure, nor the pleasure of water, of bathing, of nudity, but knew only the fraudulent pleasure of the *scourge*, of a

178

nauseating scourge. You see, we're back to where we started. It's obvious that when L.V.S. "moves in the belly of God," she comes back into the material marsh, not toward the creator god but toward the marsh where he was engulfed like the rest. And the kind of distrust I have for Georges Bataille (I had it just as much while he was alive, in spite of our good friendship), which I can't ever get rid of (a lot of us have it), is that the very premise of his research comes from a corporeal ambiguity and that the major erotic component for him is part of a blasphemous transgression. Bataille's body was that of a priest. No *idea,* nothing, can get rid of that stench: the odor permeates everything. I always see a *physical* naiveté in the people who admire Bataille (and never, never Blanchot) unconditionally. I'm talking especially about the erotic writings of Bataille, not of *Le Coupable* or *l'Expérience intérieure.* I suddenly think that maybe it's even more serious than this: that maybe Bataille didn't live this blasphemous transgression but that he used it from the outside like a theatrical device, that he played it in the writing but that he didn't get sexual pleasure from it. I can't do a single thing about this distrust, this physical reading of Bataille. If people tell me I don't *understand* him, it's because I haven't managed to express it.

71 "Then one day, this weakened body moves inside the belly of God!"

72 M.D. I don't understand this sentence about the wells, the water that they drink. As if this knowledge could be swallowed like the water, without anyone paying attention? Maybe.

73 Translator: Here, Duras first uses the formal pronoun *vous* to address Gauthier and then corrects herself, switching back to the informal *tu.* Her apology and explanation that the plural caused the confusion is based on the fact that *vous* designates both "you" singular in formal address and "you" plural in formal or informal address.

74 X.G. Right after this interview we went out into the garden, and Marguerite said to me point-blank, "You must think I'm mentally ill, don't you?" And to show her how aberrant and unthinkable this was, I said: "Are you crazy?"

75 X.G. Several days later we had a car accident that would probably have been fatal . . . had you not driven slowly.

179

Afterword

§ 1

In the Third Interview of *Woman to Woman,* Duras discusses the making of *La Femme du Gange* and relates her discovery of the "voice film": "So they spoke in all directions and . . . like birds, these voices are birds, it's like a sound of wings. They speak in all directions. I also had to . . . choose, from all that they were saying." This description offers an intriguing parallel, I think, with our reading of the Duras-Gauthier interviews, for the voice film contrasts with the image film. The two together create a "bi-film": two stories—one in words, one in pictures—which each tells something different. The voices and images, moving separately, at their own pace, break the expected unity between sound and sight, between speech and act. The listener-viewer is split, pulled in various directions by competing stimuli, by contradictory and superposable meanings. In the contradictions, multiplicity, and gaps within sound, within vision, and between them, the listener-viewer, faced with the unexpected, has the choice of taking meaning from the bi-film or of making meaning in it. This choice, whether conscious or unconscious, of taking or making meaning holds within it the promise and the threat of self-loss and self-recognition.

In her preface, Gauthier describes the interviews in a way that recalls Duras's voice film. She explains how throughout the interviews the two women's discourses overlap, contradict, ignore each other, or—as Duras might say—"speak in all directions." What is on stage, in play, here is the contrast between the spoken word and the scene of its utterance, which is carefully designated for us by bracketed explanations. The "image" thus is made present to us in the text so that, as we read, we are continually reminded of the distance separating our reading-listening of two French women's conversations from their living of those conversations. We are asked to imagine for ourselves their scene of speech, to construct a visual text to accompany the spoken-written one. We superpose our images with their voices in the creation of a "bi-text."

Their voices? Not quite. For this spoken-written text that we read is already, before the superposition of our images of Duras and Gauthier, a kind of "bi-text." The women's multidirectional discourses come to us as a *trans-script* in a double sense. The speech is not only written as spoken and acted out; it is also translated. We confront in our reading a triple slippage in meaning as it comes through language, a tri-translation: from the women's face-to-face conversations to the tape recording; from the recording to its transcription and publication, *Les Parleuses;* from *Les Parleuses* to the English translation, *Woman to Woman.* We, in our reading and responding, are engaged in a tri-textual activity. Our choices of taking meaning from, making meaning in what we read are played out in the gaps and tensions between image and speech, between words and what lies behind them, and between French and English.

These gaps and tensions, these "blanks," are characteristic of Duras's works themselves. Gauthier and Duras frequently note that the blanks take shape in silence, break up language, dislocate space and time, sound and vision, and block easy comprehension. The blanks inhibit understanding because they disturb our expectations and call into question what we think we already know. Faced with the blank, we cannot comprehend—that is, possess and master— the work. Yet conversely, as Duras says in the Fifth Interview, her stories seem to inhabit other people. She draws them out of us, of you, of me. Distinctions are blurred between writer and reader-viewer. What, then, is this transitive property, this phenomenon of translatability that seems almost inherent in the works of Duras when, at the same time, the blank supposedly blocks our comprehension?

The paradox might first be elucidated by the double meaning of the word "translation." The English word, in its common sense, means a shift from one language to another. To the extent that translation marks difference, it can also designate *explanation,* an accounting for difference. The French word for our English "translation" is *traduction.* But French also has the word *translation,* which denotes a transfer or *conveyance* of matter. By extension, it can imply a transmission and a recognition of or identification with the message being transmitted. In Duras's use of language, then, we frequently confront the blank on the level of the word or signifier such that language sounds strange, foreign. At certain points we may find ourselves doing the work of *traduction,* trying to substitute other words closer to our own vocabulary or trying to explain and account for the difference the blank signals. Yet at the same time, or at other times, we may also respond to what the blank signifies. In this case, although the signifiers may be strange, we nonetheless recognize and identify with what they seem to mean. The blank "translates" something back to us from our own experience. Thus, throughout our reading or viewing, we find ourselves both inside and outside of what Duras says and how she says it.

This inside-outside paradox and the reader-viewer's relationship to *translation* and *traduction* is intricately linked in Duras's works to the notion of desire. As Duras and Gauthier describe it in the interviews, desire is exquisite pain and occasional exhilaration. Pain, in this sense, is the extreme discomfort and frustration of being always on the edge, never quite *there,* never quite arrived, completed, or relieved. Pain is the constant deferral or displacement of release, the constant struggle for it, whether physical ("orgasm") or intellectual-psychological (the comfort of "comprehension"). The reader or viewer, like many of Duras's "characters," never quite *gets* it. Yet this "never quite," while frustrating and frightening, can be exhilarating precisely because it implies at least a partial release, a forgetfulness of the self and its limits in its distinction from the other, and of all the ordinary boundaries that keep us simultaneously safe and imprisoned. The "never quite" is the working of desire. It opens the reader-viewer to possession *by* the text, to the stories told there, to a "ravishing" by forces simultaneously external and internal to the individual. As Duras indicates in the Second Interview, desire thus conceived is a force *beyond* the person, beyond the personal. It circulates. It is not something I, you, he, she can own or master or control.

Now what does this conception of desire have to do with our reading of *Woman to Woman*? I would suggest that our desire for comprehension of the interviews doubles, to some extent, the struggle of the reader-viewer of Duras's other works. Like those works, these interviews are not always easy to understand. As Gauthier promised, they are full of detours, gaps, disjunctions. And faced with these blanks and twists, we may feel ourselves disturbed, discomfited, turned distressingly and thrillingly around by what the women are saying and how they are talking. As Gauthier and Duras explore the intersecting domains of women's experiences and feminine specificity, as they consider how Western culture has constructed woman and wonder what lies underneath or beyond those constructions, we may recognize ourselves in their discoveries or we may remain outside, separate, blocked, uncomprehending. Furthermore, the style itself of the interviews may draw us into the work because we are compelled by the image of two women talking together, by the (simulated) rhythm of their words, and because we want to speak in turn to their text, with them, against them.

On the levels of both style and content, image and text, then, we quite likely find ourselves, lose ourselves weaving in and out of what Duras and Gauthier delineate implicitly and explicitly as female and feminine terrains. To be neither always inside nor always outside is unsettling. Our uneasy relationship to *Woman to Woman* can allow us to elucidate the ways meaning is constructed, conveyed, and received. Each time we confront a blank in these dialogues, we, as American readers of the late 1980s and beyond, must wonder what accounts for the impasse: is it linguistic, cultural, historical, sexual, personal? How do we "take" this text—where is the line between the ravishing of it/by it and the raping of it/by it? What are the limits of the blank? Our very way of dealing with it, whether we let it go or fill it in with some (other) meaning, illustrates the power of the woman or man who uses or refuses speech, which is, itself, the issue at the heart of these interviews.

How do we choose what we hear from all that the women are saying?

As I suggested, what you "hear" is already a kind of bi-text, for any translation (*traduction*) is a displacement and substitution of meaning from the first text. I have necessarily made choices in relating French and American languages and cultures that will affect your reading. If my choices obscure meaning for you, this is where we could discern a limit of the blank. For I have imposed my meaning upon you; yet how can you tell that a given blank is *my* production and not Duras's and Gauthier's or your own? It is my hope that I have not abused my power as translator and that my presence, mediating between you and the women speaking, detracts as little as possible from their text. But as Duras reminds us in the First Interview, any translation risks co-option; one meaning is not always as good as another. Multiplicity and plurality still carry with them judgments and constrictions, and the notion of a "bi-text" or "tri-text" is not a release from the responsibility of conveying a message. It is your task as reader to choose to whom or to what you assign the responsibility of making meanings.

At times, then, when you confront a slippage in meaning as it comes through language, you might attribute it to the fact that these are two *French* women talking. And French and American (like French and Indochinese) *cultures* speak differently. When Gauthier and Duras talk about specific people and events, we remain more or less outside their exchanges, depending on how much we know of French history and culture. It is here, on the outside of discourse where meaning through words is effectively withheld from us, that our image-text may come most frequently into play. In our struggle to understand, we may shift from a verbal to a visual register, envisioning meaning conveyed in a glance or gesture or tone passing between two French women one summer's moment more than a decade ago.

At other points of cultural opacity or complexity, we will position ourselves around the Duras-Gauthier text verbally, doing the analytical work of *traduction* in an attempt to explain distance and difference. For example, in view of Duras's and Gauthier's descriptions of woman's eroticism and passion as a mortal wound, burning, fire, a desire impossible to satisfy, we might wonder to what extent women in America have historically lived erotic desire in the same way. Or rather, we might ask ourselves how woman's desire has been *represented* in America in literature and the visual arts and how those representations influence women's lives. These points of cultural complexity facilitate our attempt to account for a female and feminine specificity because they show how meaning, value, truth, and gender are constructions. As Gauthier and Duras strip away layers of construction, what do they and we find? Duras's numerous evocations of her childhood in Sadec and the Vietnamese girls, for example—their primitive joy and basic receptivity to nature—are attempts to mine beneath the Western version of man and his negative vision of woman. Do American women recognize something of themselves in the Vietnamese girls and their relationship to nature? Does Duras's representation "translate" a transcultural, transcendental truth to us about female sexuality? Similarly, Gauthier in the First Interview speaks of her conviction that only a woman writer could have brought the blank into view as Duras has. She suggests that a man, because of his sexuality, could not show this emptiness. Yet in other places the women consider the homosexual male writer as closer to woman and implicitly raise the dilemma of the attempt to get (back) to nature from culture.

At other points where Duras and Gauthier present us with discrepancy in meaning, we might attribute it to the fact that these are two *women* talking. Again, as Gauthier states in her preface, the women do not always follow one another in dialogue. Our question becomes, how do gaps and disjunctions characterize women's language here in the interviews and elsewhere? For example (as the two women try to discover in the Fourth Interview), what does it mean for women to talk together? Gauthier advocates a temporary female separatism in order for women to talk to each other, to find and define themselves *as women;* Duras resists this separatist imperative and advocates a political "conjunction," women making political statements to the outside and, in so doing, talking to and for each other.

In this section of the interview, Duras and Gauthier do not "resolve," conclude, or decide their differences on the questions of women's talking and under what conditions it is most effective for themselves or for society. Perhaps it is this "lack of resolve" or refusal to conclude that opens up the space, a few pages later, for the two speakers to enact in the dynamism of their discourse a kind of resolution and illustrate Gauthier's point that there are certain things women can and need to say to one another which seem to ignite an energy, empathy, and solidarity among them.

The discussion is about women's experiences of their body. In their exchange of personal histories and cultural observations about menstruation, Duras and Gauthier delimit a physical and cultural experience that is fundamental to all women in Western society. As it emerges both in and between the lines of discussion, an appreciation of this specificity can enable women to feel positive and powerful about themselves, even though patriarchy has instilled in them negative feelings of self-disgust. Duras and Gauthier do not, however, pronounce upon their discussion here; they do not *say* in the course of dialogue that their exchange has newly enabled them or that its purpose is to enable others. Instead, they leave us room to receive our own sense of empowerment and to perceive theirs. The

pace and dynamism of their discourse expresses their empowerment; it contrasts, I feel, with the more halting rhythm a few pages
earlier, where the women disagreed over the value of talking to a
man about women's bodies.

You might account differently for this discrepancy in rhythm and
what it means about women talking together. Or you might hold
Duras, for example, responsible for contradicting herself in this
instance rather than choosing to recognize and interpret those
contradictions as a struggle to rethink and reposition herself. What
is essential in your reading and my reading of these dialogues is to
respond to the women's language, to give our responses their full
range, and to describe this range for ourselves and each other so
that we do not finally read-listen-envision alone.

My original question—how do we choose what we hear from all
that the women are saying?—clearly encompasses another: how do
we speak to what we hear in the spirit of the women's dialogues? As
we listen to these two women speaking, I think we hear an
invitation and challenge to respond—to respond as fully as we can
with the pain and pleasure of pushing beyond what we already
"know" or what we expect to comprehend. If we respect the blanks
in these dialogues *both* as Duras's and Gauthier's own refusals and
deferrals of easy answers and transparent meanings for themselves
and as irresistible places for us to slip inside, intermittently to merge
with their explorations and to push against them, we may then,
indeed, construct our own bi-text to ride alongside their discourse. It
is for us to strike a balance, however difficult and difficult to
measure, between questions and answers, theirs and ours. In this
way we neither voice-over the first speakers nor mutely accept all
we are told. We hear and we (re)tell how meanings are made—lost,
transferred, shared—over time and space and gender. To be possessed of, to be possessed by the desire to be listening-talking-
reading-writing women and men is, I think, the enabling power of
the Duras-Gauthier interviews.

§11

In late winter of 1986, as this translation of *Woman to Woman* was coming to completion, Marguerite Duras was prominent in Paris on at least two counts. First, bookstores everywhere displayed posters with her picture advertising her novel *La Douleur* (1985)—which had become a best seller—along with the prizewinning *L'Amant* (1984), also still much in demand. In addition, Duras herself was engaged in a series of interviews with President François Mitterand, which were appearing in a liberal-to-Left magazine called *L'Autre Journal.* The interviews were conducted in the context of the upcoming French elections and covered areas ranging from personal histories to national and international politics, such as the Greenpeace affair. Duras writes regularly for the magazine and is on the editorial board.

Duras's popularity and high visibility at this time marked a striking contrast with the marginal status she occupied at the time of the Gauthier interviews. As she says, she was then living on her foreign royalties, while her texts—felt to be opaque and difficult—went unnoticed by the reading and viewing majority. In the twelve years since the 1974 publication of *Les Parleuses,* she had traveled from the margins to the mainstream. Moreover, she had moved from the politically subversive position evidenced throughout the Gauthier interviews to a neoconservatism, demonstrated in the Mitterand interviews by her adamant support (which, as she clarified, deviated from the position of her *L'Autre Journal* colleagues) of Ronald Reagan's raid on Libya.

If Duras has moved from Left to Right in the past decade or so, she has not moved alone. Indeed, the March 1986 French national assembly elections marked a significant swing from the 1981 Socialist victory to a rightist gain and "cohabitation," the new system of power-sharing between Left and Right coalitions. However dramatic the distance traveled to the Right in France between the 1981 and 1986 elections, it is perhaps more startling and sobering to think about the undoing of the Left in '86 from the standpoint of the reversal represented by the figure '68. I focus on this figure because it is in the aftermath of the 1968 May Movement in France that the French women's movement took on renewed vigor.[1] It is in the context of the MLF (Mouvement de Libération des Femmes) that I would like briefly to consider the Duras-Gauthier interviews.

In 1974, when *Les Parleuses* was published, the MLF had been active in various ways for four years. A seemingly vast pluralism characterized the movement; that is, issues of psychoanalysis, Marxism, Maoism, socialism, and linguistics were all part of the question of woman and power and liberation. By 1977, however, the MLF had split into at least two factions: those who allied themselves with *psychanalyse et politique,* and those who allied themselves with *questions féministes.*[2]

In very reductivist terms, the adherents of *psychanalyse et politique* were concerned in various ways with woman's psycholinguistic position in Western society. In their view, woman's and man's physical, sexual, reproductive, symbolic, and semiotic roles have always been psycholinguistic-sociosexual constructions. The possibility for thoroughgoing political change therefore lies above all in the intrapsychic realm of *écriture.* Only when women and men think and write (about) themselves and others differently, with different sets of constructions, will they *act* differently and bring about lasting social change.

Meanwhile, supporters of *questions féministes*—a name taken from the title of a journal supported by Simone de Beauvoir—were compelled primarily by the material and objective conditions of women in society. They viewed women as a class, a class subjected to particular kinds of oppression based on their traditional sexual-social roles. For them, effective political change thus depends above all on shifts in social structures that give women a material basis and position of economic power from which to think about themselves and others differently: a sort of feminism *à l'américaine.*

At the time Duras and Gauthier were holding their interviews, these issues were not yet clearly seen as containing fundamental contradictions in political strategies. According to Marcelle Marini— a professor of women's writing at the University of Paris VII, a Duras and Lacan scholar, and a feminist—*Les Parleuses* had a considerable impact upon the MLF. The interviews helped tremendously to disseminate women's issues and questions of the feminine in France. Because of *Les Parleuses,* Duras herself had a large impact on the MLF, providing a positive image of woman, the woman writer, and women's use of language. Many people, and especially women, came to know of Duras on the basis of *Les Parleuses* and began reading her other works—her "difficult" works, like *Le Ravissement de Lol. V. Stein,* which the interviews had made more understandable and accessible. *Les Parleuses* created expectations in women readers about what they would find in reading Duras, and they went to her novels for confirmation of their expectations and for empowering glimpses of themselves. By 1977, *Les Parleuses* had gained for Duras a larger reading public than ever before, on both popular and critical levels.

I was impressed, in reading the press reviews (all by men), written right after the publication of the interviews in the spring of 1974), by how positively this woman's language, staged and commented upon as it is in the interviews, was received and how highly valued. Reviews from *Le Figaro, Nouvelles Littéraires, Le Nouvel Observateur,* and *Combat*—magazines ranging from the politically conservative to the far Left—highlighted the transgressive freedom and exhilarating sincerity of Gauthier's and Duras's uncensored and unedited speech, of their silences, echoing the silence in Duras's works, of their capacity to listen—all this was ascribed to the feminine and seen as politically forceful. *Les Parleuses* and, from its explicating perspective, Duras's other works led to the revolutionary discovery that women listen-talk differently from most men in Western society and that there is power in this difference.

A commitment to this dis-covery or, rather, un-covering of a woman's language, its exploration and elaboration, led Gauthier in

1976 to found and coedit one of the many feminist journals that came out of the MLF.[3] The journal was called *Sorcières* (*Sorceresses/Witches*), and in the inaugural issue Gauthier explained the reason behind the title largely in terms of language: "Why 'Sorcières?' Because they sing. Can I hear them then? It's the capacity to listen to another kind of speech. They've wanted to make us believe that women didn't know how to talk, write, that they stammered, that they were mute. That's only because they wanted to force them to talk straight, with square words, with rectilinear sentences, within the orthodoxy. In reality, they sing lullabyes, they howl, they spasmodicize, they murmur, they yell, they moan, they are quiet and even their silence is heard." We recognize much of this from Gauthier's preface to *Les Parleuses* as well as from Duras's mention of Michelet's *La Sorcière* at the end of the Fourth Interview. The Duras-Gauthier interviews raised issues about women and language that gathered force and remained vital to French women, it would seem, until at least the early 1980s, when the Socialist government set up the Ministry for Women's Rights and raised troubling and divisive questions for the MLF about political strategies and co-option.

If *Les Parleuses* raised such issues in 1974, and with great impact, Duras's and Gauthier's were not the only female voices speaking at that time in print about the feminine. The women in Paris who have, in the 1970s and '80s, gained considerable renown in America had been writing about a woman's language for some time. In 1974, when *Les Parleuses* appeared, Luce Irigaray was publishing her doctoral thesis, *Speculum, de l'autre femme*, translated by Gillian Gill as *Speculum of the Other Woman*, (Ithaca, N.Y.: Cornell University Press, 1985). Julia Kristeva, too, was publishing her doctoral thesis, *La Révolution du langage poétique*, translated by Margaret Waller as *Revolution in Poetic Language* (New York: Columbia University Press, 1984). In 1975 Hélène Cixous's "Le Rire de la Méduse" appeared, translated by Keith and Paula Cohen as "The Laugh of the Medusa" (*Signs* 1, Summer 1976). We notice that with the exception of the Cixous article, there has been a ten-year hiatus between the French publications and their English translations. What is important about this gap is not that non-French readers in America have had access to these writers only since 1984; others of their works had been translated earlier, and American feminist scholars had begun disseminating French theories of the feminine in lectures, seminars, and publications in the mid-1970s. Rather, it is important to realize that the French context in which Kristeva, Irigaray, Cixous, Duras, and Gauthier spoke, wrote, published, and were read in 1974 differs enormously not only from the context of American feminism then and now but also from the current "postfeminist" treatment in France of the feminine and women.[4]

To take the recent popularity of Duras's *L'Amant* and *La Douleur* as an example, it does not seem to be the case that an excitement about uncovering a feminine specificity, or a commitment to exploring a new power in woman's difficult and disruptive language, accounts for the eagerness with which these novels have generally been read in France. According to a consensus of critics who devoted a 1985 issue of the literary-artistic journal *L'Arc* to Duras in the wake of these novels' success, it is precisely their accessibility to the average reader that explains their popularity. On *L'Amant* they comment: "The apparent readability of the book allows all readers access to an author traditionally viewed as difficult" (Gilles Costaz); "With *L'Amant,* as earlier with *Moderato cantabile,* Marguerite Duras has succeeded in reaching a more popular audience; it's a book read in very diverse ways" (Marcelle Marini); "In *L'Amant* . . . the public is aware of this stripping bare, this 'lowering of herself,' all the more so since the woman doing it holds an elevated position in the search for abstraction" (Françoise Py); "This time round, we witness a passage from the unsaid to the sensual where all is said. Besides, after the Goncourt Award, the public who reads such award-winning books found a story in this one that unfolds through time and space in an expected way" (Gisèle

Bremondy); "There's an autobiographical fashion right now. The book's success doesn't have to do with its real qualities, but with its referential aspect" (Madeleine Borgomano).

In other words, with *L'Amant* and *La Douleur,* Duras, after all these years, delivered something "comprehensible" to the general French reading public. All those gaps and breaks and silences that *les parleuses* talk so much about and themselves communicate through seem to be filled in. While *Les Parleuses,* like *La Douleur* and *L'Amant,* helped to make Duras and her other writings more understandable to the public, the sheer force of the 1974 text lay in its capacity to mobilize women and men—politically and person- ally—to listen and talk, think and write differently in an effort to change a repressive social power structure.

After all these shifts in France from 1974, all these filled-in gaps and political reversals, how do we in post-1986 America re-view *Woman to Woman?* We, too, have certainly taken a turn to the Right since 1968, and I believe we need to mobilize now more than ever to think, talk, and act differently in and upon our world. From our bi- textual, tri-textual constructions of meaning, let us take with us, and let us translate to others, the questions the "talking women" raise: questions about women, language, social and sexual oppres- sion, and strategies for political change.

NOTES

1. For an excellent account of the political history of the French women's movement and its emergence from the student uprisings in May 1968, see Claire Duchen, *Feminism in France: From May '68 to Mitterand* (Boston: Routledge & Kegan Paul, 1986).

2. For detailed histories of French feminism, see Elaine Marks and Isabelle De Courtivron, eds., *New French Feminisms: An Anthology* (Amherst: University of Massachusetts Press, 1980); Claire Duchen, *Femi- nism in France;* Ann Rosalind Jones, "Inscribing Femininity: French Theo-

ries of the Feminine," in *Making a Difference: Feminist Literary Criticism,* ed. Gayle Greene and Coppélia Kahn (New York: Methuen, 1985); Toril Moi, *Sexual/Textual Politics: Feminist Literary Theory* (New York: Methuen, 1985).

3. For a description and presentation of other French feminist journals, see Duchen, *Feminism in France.*

4. For some up-to-date reflections on these questions, see the 1987 issue of *Yale French Studies* on "Women and the French Literary Canon," ed. Joan de Jean and Nancy K. Miller.

Bibliography

The following is a list of Duras's and Gauthier's works to date. Each section is arranged chronologically, and English translations have been noted when available.

WORKS BY MARGUERITE DURAS

Novels ────────────────

Les Impudents. Paris: Plon, 1943.
La Vie tranquille. Paris: Gallimard, 1944.
Un Barrage contre le Pacifique. Paris: Gallimard, 1950.
The Sea Wall, trans. by Herma Briffault. New York: Farrar, Straus & Giroux, 1985.

Le Marin de Gibraltar. Paris: Gallimard, 1952.
Sailor from Gibraltar, trans. by Barbara Bray. New York: Grove Press, 1967.

Les Petits Chevaux de Tarquinia. Paris: Gallimard, 1953.

Des Journées entières dans les arbres, followed by *Le Boa; Madame Dodin; Les Chantiers*. Paris, Gallimard, 1955.
Whole Days in Trees, trans. by Anita Barrows. New York: Riverrun, 1984.

Le Square. Paris: Gallimard, 1955.
The Square, trans. by Sonia Pitt Rivers and Irina Morduc. New York: Grove Press, 1959.

Moderato cantabile. Paris: Minuit, 1958.
Moderato cantabile, trans. by Richard Seaver. New York: Grove Press, 1960.

Dix Heures et demie du soir en été. Paris: Gallimard, 1960.
Ten Thirty on a Summer Night, trans. By Anne Borchardt. New York: Grove Press, 1963.

L'Après-Midi de Monsieur Andesmas. Paris: Gallimard, 1962.
L'Après-Midi de Monsieur Andesmas, trans. by Anne Borchardt in *Four Novels: The Square; Moderato cantabile; Ten-Thirty on a Summer Night; L'Après-Midi de Monsieur Andesmas*. New York: Grove Press, 1966.

Le Ravissement de Lol. V. Stein. Paris: Gallimard, 1964.

The Ravishing of Lol Stein, trans. by Richard Seaver. New York: Grove Press, 1966.

Le Vice-Consul. Paris: Gallimard, 1965.
The Vice-Consul, trans. by Eileen Ellenbogen. London: Hamilton, 1968.

L'Amante anglaise. Paris: Gallimard, 1965.
L'Amante anglaise, trans. by Barbara Bray. New York: Grove Press, 1968.

Détruire, dit-elle. Paris: Minuit, 1969.
Destroy, She Said, trans. by Barbara Bray. New York: Grove Press, 1970.

Abahn, Sabana, David. Paris: Gallimard, 1970.
L'Amour. Paris: Gallimard, 1971.

Ah Ernesto!. Paris: François Ruy-Vidal et Harlin Quist, 1971.

Nathalie Granger, followed by *La Femme du Gange*. Paris: Gallimard, 1973.

India Song. Paris: Gallimard, 1973.
India Song, trans. by Barbara Bray. New York: Grove Press, 1976.

Le Camion, followed by *Entretien avec Michelle Porte*. Paris, Minuit: 1977.

Les Lieux de Marguerite Duras (interviews with Michelle Porte). Paris: Minuit, 1977.

Le Navire Night; Césarée; Les Mains négatives; (Aurélia Steiner; Aurélia Steiner; Aurélia Steiner.) Paris: Mercure de France, 1979.

Vera Baxter ou Les Plages de l'Atlantique. Paris: Albatros, 1980.

L'Homme assis dans le couloir. Paris: Minuit, 1980.

"Les Yeux verts." *Cahiers du cinéma* (Paris), no. 312–13, June 1980.

L'Eté 80. Paris: Minuit, 1980.

Outside. Paris: Albin Michel, 1981.

Agatha. Paris: Minuit, 1981.

L'Homme atlantique. Paris: Minuit, 1982.

Savannah Bay. Paris: Minuit, 1982; 2d ed. augmented, Minuit, 1983.

La Maladie de la mort. Paris: Minuit, 1982.

L'Amant. Paris: Minuit, 1984. *The Lover*, trans. by Barbara Bray, New York, Pantheon, 1985.

La Douleur. Paris: P.O.L., 1985.

La Musica deuxième. Paris: Gallimard, 1985.

Plays ─────────────────

Les Viaducs de la Seine-et-Oise. Paris: Gallimard, 1959. *The Viaducts of Seine and Oise*, trans. by Barbara Bray and Sonia Orwell in *Three Plays*. London: Calder and Boyars, 1967.

Théâtre I: Les Eaux et forêts; Le square; La musica. Paris: Gallimard, 1965.

L'Amante anglaise. Paris: Cahiers du TNP, 1968.

Théâtre II: Suzanna Andler; Des Journées entières dans les arbres; Yes, peut-être; Le Shaga; Un Homme est venu me voir. Paris: Gallimard, 1968. *Three Plays: The Square; Days in the Trees; The Viaducts of Seine and Oise.* London: Calder and Boyars, 1967. *Suzanna Andler; La Musica; L'Amante anglaise*, trans. by Barbara Bray. London: Calder, 1975.

L'Eden cinéma. Paris: Mercure de France, 1977.

Théâtre III: La Bête dans la jungle, based on Henry James, adaptation by James Lord and Marguerite Duras; *Les Papiers d'Aspern*, based on Henry James, adaptation by Marguerite Duras and Robert Antelme; *La Danse de mort*, based on August Strindberg, adaptation by Marguerite Duras. Paris: Gallimard, 1984.

Screenplays ─────────────

Hiroshima, mon amour. Paris: Gallimard, 1960. *Hiroshima, mon amour*, trans. by Richard Seaver. New York: Grove Press, 1960.

Une Aussi Longue Absence, in collaboration with Gérard Jarlot. Paris: Gallimard, 1961.

Films ───────────────────

La Musica, 1966.

Jaune le soleil, 1971.

Nathalie Granger, 1972.

La Femme du Gange, 1973.

India Song, 1974.

Baxter, Vera Baxter, 1976.

Son Nom de Venise dans Calcutta désert, 1976.

Des Journées entières dans les arbres, 1976.

Le Camion, 1977.

Le Navire night, 1978.

Césarée, 1979.

Les Mains négatives, 1979.

Aurélia Steiner, dite *Aurélia-Melbourne,* 1979.

Aurélia Steiner, dite *Aurélia-Vancouver,* 1979.

Agatha ou les lectures illimitées, 1981.

L'Homme atlantique, 1981.

Dialogo di Roma, 1982.

Les Enfants, 1984.

WORKS BY XAVIÈRE GAUTHIER

Surréalisme et sexualité. Paris: Gallimard, 1971.

Léonore Fini. Paris: Goldschmidt.

Rose saignée. Paris: des femmes, 1974.

La Hague, ma terre violentée. Paris: Mercure, 1981.

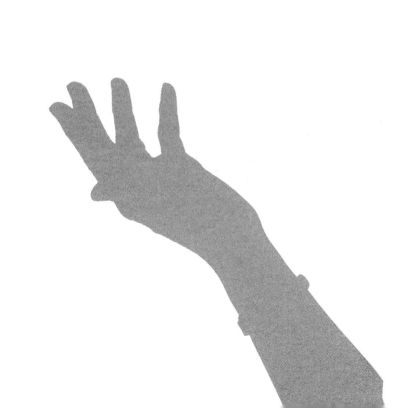